Creation's Wisdom

CREATION'S WISDOM

Spiritual Practice and Climate Change

Daniel Wolpert

ORBIS BOOKS
Maryknoll, New York 10545

Founded in 1970, Orbis Books endeavors to publish works that enlighten the mind, nourish the spirit, and challenge the conscience. The publishing arm of the Maryknoll Fathers and Brothers, Orbis seeks to explore the global dimensions of the Christian faith and mission, to invite dialogue with diverse cultures and religious traditions, and to serve the cause of reconciliation and peace. The books published reflect the views of their authors and do not represent the official position of the Maryknoll Society. To learn more about Orbis Books, please visit our website at www.orbisbooks.com.

Library of Congress Cataloging-in-Publication Data

Names: Wolpert, Daniel, 1959- author.
Title: Creation's wisdom : spiritual practice and climate change / Daniel Wolpert.
Description: Maryknoll, New York : Orbis Books, 2020. | Includes bibliographical references and index.
Identifiers: LCCN 2020006724 (print) | LCCN 2020006725 (ebook) | ISBN 9781626984011 (trade paperback) | ISBN 9781608338658 (ebook)
Subjects: LCSH: Nature—Religious aspects—Christianity. | Climatic changes—Religious aspects—Christianity. | Five agents (Chinese philosophy) | Spiritual life—Christianity.
Classification: LCC BT695.5 .W655 2020 (print) | LCC BT695.5 (ebook) |
    DDC 261.8/8—dc23
LC record available at https://lccn.loc.gov/2020006724
LC ebook record available at https://lccn.loc.gov/2020006725

For Wisdom
Who has been my lifelong guide and teacher
And who meets me in every thought

Contents

Preface

One of my earliest spiritual experiences occurred at age eleven. I was sitting in my seventh grade science class, and the teacher was explaining the structure of a cell. I can still remember the feeling, watching the drawing on the board and experiencing my mind explode. It sounds strange, I know. Yet at that moment it seemed that a great mystery was being revealed, and I knew I wanted to explore this mystery, this amazing thing at the center of most living beings. Over the next few years, I would have several such numinous encounters: when I was in the woods, when I learned about meditation, when I was alone at night.

These mystical events led me through the world of science and are what ultimately led me to embrace my vocation as a student of the spiritual life, a vocation I have pursued for over four decades.

This book has its roots in those early experiences and is the culmination of my life of contemplation and action. I am thrilled to have the opportunity to bring together many of the teachings that have been given to me and that I've been able to put into practice in spiritual communities, churches, and the healings arts.

I also find myself somewhat stunned that this book was written and produced during the COVID-19 global pandemic. That I made the decision to try and write a book about spirituality and climate change a mere six months before this worldwide catastrophe began feels like the sort of providential act that, as I often joke with friends, "almost makes you want to believe in God." If the rise of the coronavirus, as yet another catastrophe in a long list of recent climate-related catastrophes, is not enough to convince us that we need to relate to ourselves and our world differently, it is hard to imagine what will get that message through our collective consciousness. For the spiritual life is, at its heart, about learning from our experience as well as from books or traditions. And while Jesus is my primary teacher, over the years I've had hundreds of wonderful teachers and traveling companions. I endeavor to learn from each person I encounter and have often found wisdom in the most unlikely places, an experience had by many who are open to the whisper of God amid the chaos of the world.

I am grateful for the life journey I've been given, and I dedicate this work to all who seek, who journey, and who are on the Way.

Introduction

The purpose of spirituality—a term referring to the study and practice of our relationship with all that lies beyond the bounds of our individual self—is to help people make sense of the world and find their way through the difficulties of life. This has been true in every society and in every era. Faced with pain, suffering, death, confusion, joy, love, and care, people struggle to find meaning, solace, comfort, and assurance in a universe that often appears arbitrary and terrifying. The teachings and practices of the spiritual life have sought to provide this comfort and to help human beings find a path to peace and meaning. Whether the result of this journey is described as wisdom, enlightenment, salvation, happiness, being accepted by God, or being at one with the universe, we yearn to know that, as the gospel song says, "everything's gonna be alright this morning."

Furthermore, spirituality has always adapted and been transformed to fit the language, the culture, the era, and the particular challenges of the time and place in which it arises. In the ancient desert of Palestine, people poured oil on piles of stones to mark sacred places; in the Himalayas, people envisioned cosmic deities living in the clouds; in eighteenth-century European universities, people wrote confessions and catechisms; and these unique expressions spoke to the people of that age.

Today we are facing a new set of problems and challenges. We live in a globalized society, interconnected via information networks unimaginable only a few decades ago. With billions of people consuming resources at ever-increasing rates, it appears that our planet is nearing full capacity. What humans call wilderness disappeared long ago, and now we manage, or attempt to manage, every acre of the planet we call Earth. The globalization of industry, commerce, travel, and information has had a massive impact on the environment, at a scale we still struggle to accept. Global climate change is upon us with a transformative power that threatens to outstrip both our ability to understand what is happening and our ability to respond to the changes we are experiencing. These changes threaten to uproot millions of people from their homes, render large swaths of the planet uninhabitable, and perhaps even end human life on earth as it is currently constituted.

This environmental crisis has hatched, or coincides with, various crises related to our health as well as our spirituality. Throughout the world, but particularly in the First World, levels of mental illness are rising dramatically, as are the levels of chronic, lifestyle-related, physical illnesses. In 2020, the world was being gripped by the COVID-19 pandemic. Anxiety, depression, and chronic pain have become staples of the population in the United States, affecting over a third of the population. In particular, anxiety about climate change and the effects it will have on our future is becoming endemic, especially among people under forty.

At the same time, especially within this younger demographic, involvement in traditional Christianity has plummeted. This form of Christianity, largely based on an extinct metaphysics, the three-story universe of heaven, earth, and hell, and wrapped in a style of worship, community practice, and intellectual assent to creeds that make little sense to the modern person, does not speak to the fears, longings, and understandings of our twenty-first-century population. When the earth is burning, worrying about the activity of invisible deities on thrones often feels unhelpful, let alone real. Meanwhile, as traditional religious practice has waned, interest in spiritual practices—a wide variety of meditation and prayer practices that engage us experientially and lend themselves to communal interactions that are relational and loving—has increased dramatically. People are seeking a spirituality for our time.

The purpose of this book is to address that need: What would a Christian spirituality that resonates with people in an era of climate change be like? What are the practices that can help lead and guide us? What would a helpful perspective be? As we alluded to earlier, spiritualities have drawn from their environment—their time and place—to speak most clearly to their intended audience, their tribe. For people in the mountains, it would have made no sense to talk of a flat desert. For people who were discovering the logic of the Enlightenment and were enamored of words and concepts, pouring oil on rocks would have seemed absurd. For people living in a time of climate crisis, we need our focus and the attention of our faith to be on the basic elements of creation. If creation is in crisis, then our spirituality must directly engage this creation and articulate a spiritual framework that will allow us to relate to both the world and the crisis we face in a life-giving and healthy way.

In this work we will use the tools of Christian Scripture and theology seen through the lens of modern science and also engage a set of teachings that haven't been applied to the issue of modern Christian faith, the Five Wisdom, or Five Element, teachings that arise from Chinese Five Element theory and Tibetan Five Wisdom practice. Because this latter resource has never, to my knowledge, been used in Christian theological reflection, let me explain briefly my rationale for using it here. It will also be explained in more detail in the work that follows.

Throughout Christian history, communities of faith and individuals have incorporated new or different teachings to help people see Christianity from a fresh and even deeper perspective. While some decry such activity as "syncretism" and use this term negatively, the truth is that our faith would not exist as we know it without such incorporation and integration. From minor adornments such as a Christmas tree to major philosophical insights from the Greeks, from new instruments such as the organ to the arrangement of the church calendar or the art of the Celtic knot, virtually everything that forms our religious environment has, at some point, come from somewhere else. This is not a bad thing; rather, this is how God works with us, deepens our understanding, and widens our perspective.

The biblical witness contains numerous references to God acting in the created world: the Spirit blows over the waters; the earth quakes at God's command. Wisdom is beside God creating the world and delighting in both the creation and the wisdom that creates, and the power of God is manifest in the created order. However, despite this obvious intertwining of creation and the Divine, the Christian relationship between the human being and the universe has become alienated and distorted by the idea that humans are separate from and meant to dominate "nature."

Our relationship with the natural world and our faith has also suffered from the denigration of "natural theology," that is, any theological system that relies on nature for any of its observations and conclusions. This dislike of natural theology has arisen, particularly in Protestant circles, from the emphasis on *sola scriptura* (Scripture alone). This phrase implies that it is only through Scripture, the Bible, that we can know anything about God and that any conclusions drawn from nature must be inherently misleading at best or nature-worshiping paganism at worst. This rejection of natural theology is misguided and even antiscriptural. There are myriad stories in the Bible where people come to understand, hear, know God through nature. As we will discuss throughout this book, the wisdom tradition of the Bible is intimately bound up with the natural world and our experience of it. Furthermore, people throughout history have always seen and experienced God through God's natural world. Of course, the Bible is the central piece of written teaching that grounds and creates the Christian faith and religion. However, that doesn't mean that we do not also learn about God from the natural world; we clearly do, and the Bible promotes this learning and relationship.

Many have talked about and discussed the problem of Christian alienation from nature; and when one perspective or one set of theological habits causes us to be stuck, blocked from growth and unable to move forward in a healthy way, it is valuable to introduce another view, a different perspective. This helps us to shift and see our difficulties and challenges from a new angle, in a new light; and thus inspired and refreshed, we can continue along our path to growth and life. Bringing these ancient teachings on elemental reality into contact with Christianity, especially as they are extremely congruent with our Christian theology, will add such a new vantage point and allow us to move forward in a manner that is constructive and liberating.

The book is loosely divided into three parts: an analysis of our current condition and the new perspective that is arising; a description and discussion of the Five Wisdom teachings and practices and how this informs a spirituality for our time; and, finally, a section on how these new teachings engage our current crises and can transform our lives, our view, our practice, and our individual and collective response to a world amid climate change. Throughout, particularly in the second and third parts of the book, we will focus on spiritual practice. We are not merely interested in intellectual reflection, helpful as that can be, but rather in how we can practice our faith, do the work of contemplation, and dwell in the deep stillness of our being, where we find our connection to the source of life.

Chapters 1 and 2 examine the nature of our current environmental crisis and its intersection with the multiple other challenges we currently face. This awareness of intersectionality—understanding that all challenges and crises are linked and bound up in one another—must become clearer in our collective consciousness. Just as the stuff of the universe is interrelated and interchangeable, so too is the stuff of human life: one challenge cannot be isolated from another.

Chapter 1 describes how the crisis of climate change has rapidly broken upon us over the past three decades. Going from an emerging situation that few recognized in its early stages to a worldwide transformational force, global warming has arrived as the central issue of our time. Yet it is not the only global phenomenon that plagues humanity. Issues of chronic health problems, addiction, human displacement, and other environmental challenges resulting from our consumerist lifestyle threaten to overwhelm us.

The second chapter examines how these issues share a spiritual root: our alienation from the rest of "nature." Although human beings are inseparable from the rest of creation, the Christian approach to our relationship with the rest of the natural world has far too often understood humanity as a separate and superior entity that can do with nature what it wills without consequence. Additionally, our lack of training in the awareness and management of change and transformation, and our deep attachments to "the way things are," has left us with an unconscious assumption that the material world is immutable and immune to the forces of chaos, death, and resurrection. Essentially, we assume that the sun will rise and set every day, that spring will follow winter, and that the worship schedule at our local church will never change.

This disconnection from the way things are—a form of delusional thinking—has led to a series of collective actions that then manifest our errors of perception and relationship via the crises we are experiencing. Yet, despite these errors, ecological systems are self-correcting and often contain the cure for what ails them; and at this exact juncture where we are being threatened by our alienated states, a great yearning for spiritual practice and deep reconnection has arisen within human society.

The third chapter explores the nature of this spiritual awakening and, in particular, how it has evolved to focus on embodied spiritualities that reveal our desire to cure our traumas, our embodied disconnections, and reroot us in our relationship with creation. These movements, many of which highlight the indigenous roots of the spiritual life, can be of great help as we seek a spirituality for our time. This chapter, which makes the explicit case for the need of an elemental spirituality, will lead directly to the descriptions of the Five Elements.

Chapters 4 through 9 describe the Five Element/Wisdom perspective, how it applies to and integrates with the Christian faith, and also how it brings us closer to the natural world and provides a framework for seeing wisdom no matter what the future brings. Each chapter also contains a practice component in keeping with this contemplative approach.

Arising from the ancient Chinese Five Element theory, the Five Wisdom teachings begin with a perspective confirmed by modern science, namely, that everything in the universe is interrelated and interdependent. Furthermore, it understands, like the Hebrew biblical tradition, that wisdom is present in

xviii   Introduction

creation at all levels of existence and that our job, as humans, is to listen for this wisdom and "walk in the way of insight" (Proverbs 9:6).

Christian theology has described the human condition as being fundamentally confused in our relationship to the Divine—a condition commonly known as original sin—and has also affirmed the central role of creation in God's actions in this universe. However, much like the elusive search for a unified field theory in physics, Christianity has struggled to find an elegant and life-giving integration of its descriptions of the human being, creation, the divine life, and salvation, the overcoming of confusion. The Five Wisdom teaching can aid us in achieving this deep integration and thus allow us to practice immersing ourselves in both our relationship with God and the creation such that we can find paths to health and wholeness.

The Five Wisdom teaching sees the five elements—space, water, earth, fire, and air—not just as physical elements but as holistic expressions of psychological and spiritual realities, what Christians understand as the attributes of God. Thus, each element contains an inherent wisdom that manifests both internally within each organism and also externally in creation: in seasons, landscapes, and cultures. This wisdom, or spiritual energy, is available to everyone and unites everyone as it flows, much like the divine breath, through time and space.

Human beings, as creatures with the capacity for individual awareness—one of the distinctive signs of the divine image we are said to possess—have the ability to relate to these elemental energies from either a wisdom or a neurotic perspective. When we let go of our ego self and allow wisdom to arise naturally, we experience the qualities of wisdom, or the presence of God; but when we are in relationship with an element from our ego perspective, we experience the neurotic manifestation of that element.

The five chapters dealing with each individual element detail the wisdom and neurotic aspect of each energy and also describe how we shift from the neurotic experience of separateness and control to the wisdom experience of healing and integration. Beginning with the wisdom of *space*, we will explore the nature of the loving container God has given us, a reality that can support and hold the vast array of biological systems that we call life on earth. Next we will see how the wisdom of *water* provides for us the clarity we need to see what is happening to us and to reality and then make wise decisions as we move forward in our individual and collective lives. The wisdom of *air* guides these compassionate actions, for air is the element of movement and accomplishing things in the world. Next, the wisdom of *earth* shows us that we can be grounded in abundance; God is always providing enough, and thus we can choose actions that create an environment of sharing, hospitality, and bounty without exploitation of people or resources. Finally, the wisdom of *fire* binds us together in loving relationship and gives us the capacity to experience love in all its dimensions as we relate to ourselves, each other, and God.

Following this detailed discussion and description of the elemental approach, the final four chapters engage in a series of reflections on the practical ramifications of an elemental faith. Central to each of these discussions is the previously noted deep realization that life is elemental and intertwined. In considering the environment, people, animals, plants, and society, we realize they are made of the same "stuff" as we are. Furthermore, this stuff has been in dynamic relationship with itself, changing places from one creature and object to another. Seeing and embodying these truths, we can no longer abide any theological, philosophical, or sociopolitical system that treats the "other" as different from ourselves. It is this deep awareness of connection that guides us to a new way of being in a time of climate change.

Building on this central insight, these chapters will assist readers in examining their own elemental histories, both in terms of what is our dominant energy or element and also in terms of our deeper history with wisdom and neurosis: How have we internalized an alienated approach to creation through our religion, our culture, and our interaction with a variety of oppressive systems? What in our history has kept alive a tradition of wisdom? How we can connect profoundly with this wisdom, one that brings us more fully into alignment with God's work in the world and creates a relationship to our current condition that fosters healing?

The final two chapters address the issue of despair: how can we face the existential crisis that is upon us? An elemental faith is one that understands and lives in the reality of impermanence and transformation. Our spiritual lives and practices can help us live in the reality of change, let go of fear, and cease grasping for permanence. Our Christian faith tells us that God is in all things and that our relationship with the divine person of Jesus grounds us in the experience of eternity. Unfortunately, while many claim to "believe" these statements, our lives rarely reflect this belief; and it is hard to see concrete manifestations of a fearless connection to God in day-to-day existence. Hopefully, as we see and practice the dance of elemental wisdom, we can experience directly our connection to the vast spiritual reality that is God and learn to be in creation while knowing a boundless love that sustains us, no matter what comes next.

As we embark on this elemental journey, note that this work draws from various sources and disciplines as well as my entire life of experience, study, and contemplative practice. One option for such a work is an academic approach with a huge set of footnotes, a myriad of cited sources, and a large dose of quotes from others. Such a style is extremely valuable and also, frankly, inaccessible to the majority of people. Rather, I have chosen to adopt a more readable approach that is accessible to a wide audience. References have been provided in the footnotes for further investigation, and, of course, we have the internet, where information about anything is available with a few keystrokes.

Furthermore, I have chosen not to address the issue of the "truth" of the variety of teachings presented here. I realize that there are people who do not think God exists or do not believe in the tenets of the Christian faith, just as there are those who do not believe in the precepts of Chinese medicine or Buddhism. I have no quarrel with anyone who dismisses these disciplines. My own epistemological stance to spiritual teachings is not one of "blind" belief but rather the skeptical approach of a scientist: the value of a theory or set of teachings is not whether they are objectively "true," as every theory falls short in this regard, but whether it helps us to navigate the world. When the response is yes, then the theory is worthwhile; when the answer becomes no, or a better theory comes along, then the theory is no longer "true" or worth keeping. Therefore, having engaged and studied the teachings outlined in the following pages for my entire adult life, I find them to be "true" because I find them to be helpful and healing as we pursue peace, justice, and a world with less suffering.

1

The Earth Has a Fever

Humanity has arrived at a difficult juncture. After several hundred thousand years of growth and development, the past one hundred years has seen profound and unprecedented growth. Worldwide human population explosion, along with a technological explosion, has brought changes few could have imagined; and with these changes have come unique crises and challenges.

Many people have stopped listening to the news because it has become too hard and provokes too much anxiety. We are overwhelmed by what is happening around us, both immediately and on a planetary scale. These feelings are understandable, and our purpose here is to address both the realities that confront us and our responses to them.

While technology and society have undergone these recent massive transformational changes, our religions, institutions, and communities, which are supposed to offer help and guidance during challenging times, have remained largely unchanged, choosing stagnation over new life.

In the late 1990s, when I was in the seminary, a professor told a story about how the seminary brought in a consultant to help develop its curriculum. He gathered the faculty together and drew a vertical line on a white board, creating two columns. He then asked the faculty to list the changes in society from

the 1960s to the 1990s. The observations came fast and furi-
ous, and soon one column was full of the new things that had
happened in the world. Next, he asked the faculty what had
changed in the seminary curriculum in this same period of
time. The answer was that nothing had changed. The second
column remained empty.

While the current decline in established religion has multiple
causes, one of them is that an eighteenth-century religion cannot successfully speak to a twenty-first-century world in crisis.
We need new ways to imagine and engage our faith so as to face
our current reality with courage, wisdom, and insight. Descriptions of our current situation can be hard to hear, in particular,
thoughts of a planet whose ecosystems are on the verge of collapse can be terrifying. However, the teachings of the spiritual
life tell us that, in order to encounter wisdom, we must face
everything straight on; healing and goodness are found only via
an unflinching look at reality.

THE COMING CRISIS

In 1988, my wife, Debra, and I began a year-long spiritual pilgrimage around the world. Heading west from Los Angeles, we
traveled Down Under to New Zealand and Australia and then
made our way across South Asia to England, eventually arriv-
ing in Montreal. Our focus was on visiting spiritual communities, engaging in volunteer work, and trying to be pure tourists
as little as possible. We traveled on what now seems to me an
impossibly small budget, although when I think of some of the
places we stayed and the various creatures we encountered in
our hotel rooms, I'm glad we didn't pay more.

On reflection, it is hard to believe how much the world has
changed in just over thirty years. The World Wide Web, the

internet, didn't exist as a public phenomenon. When we were in Australia trying to contact our work connection in Indonesia, we were told that there was this new thing called email and we should try that rather than sending a telegraph. We laughed, tried for three days, and then sent a message in that bizarre, arcane, telegraph language full of the word "stop." Communication with our friends and family in the United States was done via blue international mailing letters, intricately folded, tabs carefully licked and sealed. Cell phones and personal computers were dreams over the horizon. The idea that it was bad not to know where someone was and to not be able to get in touch with them immediately didn't even occur to people because such connection was simply impossible. All of life was unplugged. But not for long.

On this journey, we visited ancient shrines, saw the archeological site where Java Man was unearthed, sat with people interested in deepening their spiritual lives, worked side by side with those attempting to forge new, decent, just lives, and saw the myriad of ways that humans, trying to make sense of our experience, engage and practice faith and religion. Connecting with local communities in work/mission settings was fruitful as it allowed us entry into different lands and cultures that would never have been possible as a tourist. And everywhere we went people commented—unsolicited on our part—that strange things were happening with the weather.

Another vast difference between 1988 and today is that climate change was not a public topic. Conversation about global warming was developing within scientific communities and environmental activist communities, but if you were to ask the average politician of any party, or the average person on the street, if humans were changing the climate they would either stare at you blankly or laugh. It was a preposterous notion.

And yet, here we were in the Papua Highlands being told that it was becoming just a bit warmer and that the mosquitos that carried malaria were now being seen above 7,000 feet—something unknown until that time. Then, on the east coast of India we were in a light rain during the dry season, and someone said that the rains were coming at odd times. And in the foothills in Nepal, the snow was melting earlier. At every stop, common people were noticing that something was shifting.

We've all had that feeling just before we fall ill with a cold or flu, when we feel slightly odd. There's a funny ache in our joints or our head feels foggy. We don't feel sick exactly, but we know that something isn't quite right. I have a few remedies that I can take if I pay attention to these early warning signals; and most of the time, when I do, I either don't get sick or I have a very mild illness that quickly leaves. However, if I ignore these signs, I risk ending up in bed feeling ill for a few days.

Thirty years ago, the collective human organism was noticing that something was off, was odd. The environment wasn't feeling well, wasn't operating properly. Each one of our observations, by itself, was barely a blip on the ecological radar; but taken together they were a sign that a "flu" was coming. And in response to these early warning signs, humanity did next to nothing. Like people who pretend they aren't sick, we marched on, many not even willing to admit that there is a problem. And now we are in a full blown illness—the earth has a fever.

The Climate Crisis Is upon Us

I first moved to the northern latitudes of the United States in 1987, a year before our worldwide pilgrimage. We were renting a very funky hippie-era house in Maine, just outside Augusta, where Debra was doing her second year of medical residency. Following our international journey, we returned to New

England, settling in central Vermont, first at the southern tip of Lake Champlain and then, a year later, moving to our farm in the White Mountains in the south central part of the state.

In those years, winter in that part of the country lasted for nine months. I could count on not having to mow my lawn after Labor Day as the fall frost and snow would stop it from growing, and the last frost date was Memorial Day weekend. It wasn't unusual for us to have months of sub-zero weather—one year we got three inches of snow in early June.

In 2000, when we moved to Minnesota, which is similar in latitude and climate to New England, we found basically the same weather patterns. However, by then, the news and reality of climate change was far more widespread than it was in 1988. Anyone who wasn't in complete denial knew that something was wrong with the earth's climate, and something very different was developing. We have now arrived at that distant future.

In just nineteen short years, winter in the north is now completely different from then. Today, I regularly mow my lawn well into the fall. Winter in the north is about three months long now. The last frost sometimes comes in March, and it's not unusual for it to be in the seventies in November. While we still have a number of days where it is below zero, it's rare for that to last more than a week. Interestingly, these changes have been so dramatic that people seem to have already forgotten what winter used to be like and often complain if we have a weekend that's double digits below zero, something that regularly happened for a month at a time.

Climate change is no longer a whisper, as it was in the 1980s, but rather a great shout. Not a day passes without a new article, news story, or prediction on the subject. Whether it is the ice melting, the seas rising, the changing patterns of heat and wet and dry, the effects of this worldwide illness is fully upon us. In a few decades, we have gone from thinking that climate change is impossible to hearing predictions of the complete collapse of our ecology and an uninhabitable planet within a decade.

The human response to these events and this new reality have been highly varied. Ranging from the mobilization of new technologies and new ways of living in the world to total denial and a stubborn refusal to do anything, people, as individuals, communities, and societies, have responded to the climate crisis the way that people respond to any crisis. Some engage the challenge and try to do something about it; others put their head in the sand and do nothing; and many are too busy trying to survive and simply continue to live their lives hoping for the best. On a governmental level, most countries, at least grudgingly, accept that this crisis is real and that something needs to be done either to prevent it from getting worse or to prepare for whatever may come. However, despite this general acknowledgment of the challenge we face, total human carbon emissions continue to rise; we have not found a way to halt or even significantly slow the basic cause of these changes.

The psychological effect of the climate crisis on people around the world is dramatic and painful. I regularly hear that people are staying up at night worrying about climate change; the potential for significant disaster in the decades to come is causing depression and chronic anxiety. For those who live in places where the worst effects of global warming are already being felt, the stress, of course, is much worse. It has become a regular summer ritual to wonder which major city in the world is going to run out of water and become uninhabitable. In 2018, it was Cape Town, South Africa. In 2019, it was Chennai, India. For people in these places, the mental strain results in nervous breakdowns and civil unrest. At some point, a city with millions of people will run out of water, creating a migration wave that will dwarf the current migrant issues facing places like Europe and the United States and reveal another important truth; the climate crisis is at the nexus of several intersecting crises facing humanity at this critical juncture in our evolution.

INTERSECTING CRISES

The image of global warming as a fever helps us to understand that the climate crisis is connected to numerous other health-related challenges facing humanity. Climate change as a reaction to human activity doesn't occur in a vacuum; it is connected to other societal modes of existence, revealing a web of illness and disease that is slowly smothering our planet. Here, we will briefly note several of them before we consider how they are fundamentally related to a spiritual crisis that we must address if we are to see our way to a new reality.

The earth is drowning in litter. Go to any beach in the world, no matter how remote, and you will find bits of plastic everywhere along the shore, dotting the beach like so many tiny dots of colored death. At the mouth of the Guatemala River, there is a windrow of garbage that is four feet tall and nearly ten miles long. The great garbage island in the northern Pacific is the size of Texas. I could go on for pages, but my guess is that most of you have your own stories or internet articles relating to the massive amount of waste that humans have produced and dumped somewhere. Our economic system, which is focused on consumption and excretion, is designed to produce new things constantly and requiring that the old be thrown away.

In some parts of the world, countries have made strides at reducing their waste and opting for truly recyclable products. But, like carbon emissions, the worldwide picture is of ever-increasing amounts of garbage that now has nowhere to go but into the land and sea, clogging the ecosystem, and creating filth and disruption to biological processes. Of course, this crisis of litter is directly connected to the climate crisis, for it is the production and use of this endless stream of products that produces much of the heat trapping gases in our atmosphere.

Globally, we are also facing numerous new health crises. In the United States, and much of the global north, this crisis is paradoxical. On the one hand, people are living longer than ever (although there now has been a slight downward tick in life expectancy in the United States); and so, based on the medical perspective of the 1950s that considered illnesses such as infectious diseases to be the primary cause of death, it appears that we are healthier. However, as we are living longer, we are also witnessing the rise of chronic illnesses traced to environmental and lifestyle-related issues. Furthermore, we are experiencing a steep rise in the rates of mental-health-related issues, especially among teenagers and young adults, as well as a rise in substance abuse and addiction, particularly to prescription pain killers.

These new chronic health problems are often autoimmune in nature, in that our bodies are literally attacking themselves. As our environment fills with synthetic chemicals and as our chronic stress levels increase, our immune systems do not recognize our own bodies as friendly but rather as an enemy, something to attack. Like the changes in the planet, our way of life is causing our embodied home to become unrecognizable and inhospitable.

The COVID-19 pandemic, while not a chronic illness, is yet another example of such a health crisis. Unstable ecosystems regularly produce new infectious diseases which then decimate their hosts who have no immunity to the new pathogen.

The stresses of climate change also manifest in our state of mind as life feels overwhelming and unmanageable. The speed of life and the drive to achieve, or survive, is causing higher rates of pain and mental illness. It is estimated that in the United States, a hundred million people, close to a third of the population, suffer from chronic pain and related illnesses. These conditions, in turn, drive the massive opioid epidemic, which is now causing close to seventy thousand deaths per year and several times that number of nonlethal overdoses.

A third set of crises are those related to social unrest. As already alluded to, climate change, as well as the other environmental stressors we are experiencing, is creating significant strain on our social fabric. The manifestations of these problems include war, sectarian violence, the collapse of entire countries—the so-called failed states—famine, and massive displacement. Currently, the global refugee population is estimated to be nearing a hundred million. The past several years have witnessed the mass migrations to Europe from the destabilized countries of Syria, Iraq, Afghanistan, Yemen, and Somalia, among others; the migration of a million people from Venezuela; and tens of thousands moving north from Central America. These internal displacements will only grow larger as oceans rise, rainfall patterns shift, and summer heat increases.

These patterns of displacement, war, and violence, along with the rise of anxiety, have fueled the rise of nationalism and authoritarianism as people and countries draw inward and try to protect themselves from the perceived threat of other countries. This trend is causing us to waste trillions of dollars on weapons rather than use these resources to help us respond to the crises we face, creating a downward spiral that results in more tragedy. Here we see the ego-driven, tribal response to threat: we are scared and we react by withdrawing as we try to protect ourselves. At first this approach appears helpful, but soon it yields more suffering.

WHERE DO THESE CRISES MEET?

The previous section described these crises as intersecting, and this is the concept of intersectionality noted in the introduction. The geometric image these terms conjure up is a series of lines that cross at one point, or more if the lines are curved. Intersecting lines cross because they have something in common, one place where they are the same. So what do these crises share, what is causing them to arise simultaneously?

The term "spirituality" can be defined in many ways, and I offered a brief definition earlier, but all definitions speak of relationships, usually the relationship of people or a person to something other than themselves. This "Other" is often referred to as God, but it has many names: enlightened mind, the universe, nature, spirits, etc. Spiritual teachings generally describe how the relationship between the human being and this Other— viewed as good and valuable—can be healthy and positive or unhealthy and negative. Again, the particulars of these descriptions are numerous and vary over time and cultures. The practices of spirituality are activities that help the human being move in the direction of a healthy relationship with this Other and with themselves. In the Christian tradition, the spiritual life is described as the life of prayer; and as a person and community live this life, they are able to experience the presence of God.[1] As this relationship with God deepens, God's loving presence helps us to live in harmony with the divine wish for goodness and wholeness throughout creation. Such harmony and wholeness—a state of cosmic Oneness—is the nature of the

---

1. A healthy spiritual life assumes an image of God that is positive and healthy. Those who have been exposed to a violent image of God may not want to experience such a God. I will discuss the issue of religious trauma in later chapters.

life within the kingdom of God, the biblical term for a creation in harmony with the Divine.

Considering the list of current crises, they are crises of relationship; instead of a relationship characterized by wisdom and health, we have relationships haunted by death and disorder. The human being is suffering from diseased relationships with the environment, with our eco-systems, with our own bodies, and with one another. Thus, the point of intersection of these crises is spiritual, and these calamities are, at their root, a reflection of a spiritual crisis.

In the next chapter, we examine the nature of this fundamental disease; what is it about our spiritual state that is producing the climate crisis, among others?

2

A Spiritual Crisis

As noted in the previous chapter, underlying our current climate crisis lies a corresponding spiritual crisis. This chapter explores this assertion further to understand how we got to where we are and to ascertain the solutions even as the problems deepen. To say that the root cause of our climate calamity is spiritual is, as noted earlier, to assert that it's a problem with our relationships with the universe: with ourselves, one another, and the rest of reality, which, for Christianity and other theistic religions, includes God. To explore the nature of these disordered relationships and the various views and habits that keep the relationships from being healthy, we begin with a brief reflection on dinosaurs.

Did God Kill the Dinosaurs?

People love dinosaurs. I'm tempted to say that everyone loves them, but I'm sure that's not true. We love them so much that we spend millions of dollars digging up their bones and displaying them in beautiful museums. We love them so much that we spend billions making and watching movies that depict bringing them back to life. Dinos are just "cool." They were big majestic creatures who look weird and amazing, and they are now gone.

We now posit that they were killed when the ecology changed after a massive asteroid struck the earth,[1] and while we may know and state this as a historical fact, we rarely ask: *What does this event tells us about the nature of life and change and the Spirit?* Most people would never say that God intentionally killed the dinosaurs, but what is the relationship between our material existence and our spiritual existence? Furthermore, I have noticed a distinctly different response to the fact of dinosaur extinction and the current wave of extinctions facing the planet. While the ancient extinctions are met with little emotion and acceptance, discussions of the current extinctions are often highly emotional and laced with judgment and blame. What's going on here?

The dinosaurs, their disappearance, and our reaction to their vanishing can teach us a great deal about the difference between a faith whose relationships are alienated and one whose are not; and the Christianity that most people practice and grew up with is one that is profoundly alienated when it comes to its relationship with the natural world. So let us now consider the origins of this alienated faith.

Developing an Alienated Christianity

As we observe how human beings live on the planet today, it's clear that we treat the nonhuman world, what we often call "nature," as a commodity. Even though we are made of the same atoms as the rest of nature, and even though we share highly intimate relationships with food, air, and water, we treat nature as something separate that can be manipulated, sold, bought,

---

1. The Chicxulub impactor had an estimated diameter of ten kilometers (6.2 mi) and delivered an estimated energy of 21 to 921 billion Hiroshima A-bombs (between 1.3×10^{24} and 5.8×10^{25} joules, or 1.3–58 yottajoules).

and transformed without any regard to how this affects us and our world. This relationship is in a state of alienation: we and nature have become alien to one another. Nature isn't a part of us; it's a commodity to be used.

Signs of such alienation are everywhere. Our economic system, for example, has a commodities market, where raw materials and food stuffs are bought and sold. The entire global capitalist economy is based on extracting these raw materials, often by force or exploitation, using them to create products that are sold at a profit and then, eventually, thrown away so that it costs the original maker nothing. Furthermore, activities like tourism are predicated on viewing and experiencing nature at a slight distance as if seen through a screen or a cage. If nature is too itchy, bites us, or eats us, we become irritated and angry. Thus, we need signs in the "wilderness" that tell us not to feed the animals, or that the ocean waves might knock us over, or that we shouldn't go too near the edge of the cliff because we could fall and die. How else other than as alienated could we possibly describe our relationship with the rest of the natural world when every year hundreds of people die taking selfies as they fall off the edge of a precipice?

Since the current global systems that encourage such alienation arose out of European Christian society, we must first examine the religious teachings of that society to understand our current state. Thousands of pages have been written about Genesis 1:26, in which God says that the human being has "dominion" over the creatures of the earth. Generally, the debate concerns whether this statement describes a relationship of mutuality and care or one of domination. Many see that our current systems of exploitation and alienation have been defended by those who understand the human place in creation as being separate and special from the rest of the earth, and thus giving us freedom to do with it as we want. There is much truth in this assertion; and while there is value in these reflections on the description of the human's place in creation, we need to reflect deeper and combine them with an understanding of the human being and our separate ego self, which is presented in Genesis 2.

Once humans eat of the tree of knowledge, they become aware of themselves as separate entities. This is the basic process of ego formation: as we grow from infancy we come to learn that we are distinct beings, and we develop a unique understanding of ourselves and the world around us. In fact, this ego-formation process, which we examine in greater detail in chapter 4, is what creates our particular understanding and view of reality. Thus, we experience ourselves as alive and different from the world, and we also come to understand that we can die, a discovery that generates great fear and concern. All spiritual teaching speaks of this process of ego formation and the confusion, suffering, and attachment it creates. As noted earlier, Christianity refers to this basic confusion as original sin.

Because we want to maintain ourselves forever, and you can see this in the multibillion dollar life-extension business, humans work to develop social, cultural, and religious systems that validate our desire for life and keeping our fear of death at bay. These are the tribal groups that people form, and one can see this tribalism throughout history from the earliest communities of nomads to the internet tribes we spontaneously create and inhabit.

Alienated Christianity is just such a tribal reality, and the impulse for this type of religious system wasn't one particular passage of Scripture and its errant interpretation. Rather, it was the much more basic, universal, process of ego formation. This process hijacks every spiritual teaching and breaks the heart of every spiritual teacher. The cruel paradox of an alienated faith is that the religion that is supposed to lead us out of the more basic alienation that comes from the ego process is itself hijacked by that process and used to further our confused state. No matter how many times Jesus speaks of the need to let go of self, we continue to ignore that particular prescription and use the resurrection, and a triumphalist interpretation of Jesus coming back to life, as a sign that Christians deserve to dominate the world and exploit it. Thus, over the centuries, individual and corporate egos—the social systems of church and state—took the idea of dominion and used it to validate the notion that it is okay, even God's will, for people to do what they want with the natural world, to use it to serve our need for increased comfort and life.

This ideology applied not only to nonhuman nature but also to humanity itself. Thus, the idea that one group, or tribe, is superior to another is simply part of the same process of ego maintenance and development. If my group is better than yours, and thus also more beloved by God, then slavery, colonialism, and all forms of imperial domination can be justified. In the United States, it was such an ideology, which has its origins in European colonial society, that led to the creation of the "white" class of people who were allowed to dominate nonwhite people either through extermination or slavery.

Thus we can see how alienated Christianity both developed and has led humans to a state of global alienation. The terrible problem, of course, is that a religion, a society, and a global economic system built on the ego's insatiable appetite for existence is doomed because it is based on a set of false premises—the delusions of the ego's view of reality.

The first delusion is that each ego self is separate from the world. The second is that it is possible to solidify reality and create a state of permanence. In other words, we falsely believe that we can prevent change and can maintain the status quo. And the final one is that God is on the side of our ego, but nothing could be further from the truth.

Let us now return to our friends the dinosaurs to glimpse a new perspective on the universe we inhabit.

AN IMPERMANENT REALITY

We know how different it can be to view something difficult from a detached perspective, and often we feel guilty about this difference. When we are detached from something, it has less of an impact on us; we are not as distressed by tragedy or excited by success if we are not involved. For example, we hear about a tragedy and may feel uncomfortable when we think, "I'm glad that wasn't me or my loved ones." When disaster strikes, we are on edge until we know our family is safe, and then we can feel our bodies relax and the adrenalin subsides. This experience is another example of our ego self, and its focus on self-maintenance, at work. Rather than judge ourselves negatively for these reactions, what can we learn from them?

Evolution is a model that describes how creation happened and how beings are formed. It is elegant and beautiful in many ways, and those who love it, myself included, appreciate its vision of a kaleidoscopic movement of forms. Yet, we do not experience the effects of the evolutionary processes directly; we haven't seen massive evolutionary change in our human lifetimes. The vast majority of it took place in a time when none of us were in existence, and even the more recent eras involved people with whom we have no emotional connection. Thus, we are detached from the process of evolution, and this detachment prevents us from understanding the changes involved in this mechanism of creation more deeply.

For those who subscribe to the notion of God, we understand that God is somehow involved in the evolutionary process.[2] Theologically, we say that God is involved in creation,
both initially and in an ongoing basis. We also ascribe to God
certain emotional states such as love, caring, compassion, and
anger, among others. These two theological assertions are combined when we hear that God delights in Wisdom as they create
together (see Proverbs 8:30–31), and we can, therefore, imagine that God has loved and appreciated all beings, animate and
inanimate, that have existed over the years. God probably loved
the dinosaurs as much as anyone. And yet, God also seems to
have been perfectly fine with them being wiped out by a meteor
in order to give rise to a new ecology dominated by mammals,
whom God also loves.

When we hear about this process of evolutionary change, and
we see it from our detached vantage point, we generally do not
feel that there is a problem with the flow of life throughout the
ages. We don't rail at God for killing the dinosaurs. We don't
get upset that the earth is no longer dominated by algae, pro-
tozoans, or inanimate objects. Rather, we understand that deep
change is a fundamental aspect of our universe, and we recognize that things come and go, and that God must be fine with
such transformations because material forms are impermanent;
matter and energy are conserved, and everything is just a dance
of matter and spirit.

When it comes to our own period, however, we suddenly have
a very different set of reactions. If we listen carefully to the conversations about the climate crisis, we can hear two important
themes. The first one is that we are not in a good position with

---

2. For a detailed discussion of God in evolution, see Daniel
Wolpert, *The Collapse of the Three Story Universe: Christianity in an
Age of Science* (Crookston, MN: MICAH, 2013), 21–29.

the changes that are happening. As mentioned earlier, people are experiencing numerous physical- and mental-health-related issues that are connected to our fear and uncertainty as we face the climate crisis.

The second important theme is that our alienated perspective on nature is revealed in how we discuss the role of human beings in climate change; and this occurs even when we talk about *not* being alienated from the natural world. Thus, we say things like, "Humans are causing another great extinction, and that's different from other 'natural' extinctions." Or we project our anger and judgment on humanity for the current climate crisis as if we are doing something "unnatural" to "nature." Yet, we are part of the natural world, as is our ego process!

If we have arrived at our current condition, with its problems and crises, and we wish to address these challenges from a holistic, nonalienated state, then we must face them, accepting that everything, any event, any activity, any change, is a part of nature and that God is with us in all that occurs. From an ecological perspective, this wholistic approach indicates an understanding of the dynamics of change and crisis in natural systems. For our purposes we must highlight two themes related to change that are central to our undertaking.

The first is that such moments of massive transformation, while certainly difficult to appreciate when we consider what is passing away, are also moments of openness when something new and exciting is forming. We can certainly project our care and concern onto the individual dinosaurs who suffered when the earth's ecosystem was radically thrown into a state of chaotic disequilibrium. Although nonhuman creatures probably suffer differently than humans, given that they have a different self-awareness, there was probably much suffering as the climate morphed and cooled and various species became extinct. Nevertheless, the dinosaurs of one kind or another were around for hundreds of millions of years—not bad for a given group of created beings.

Our ego attachment to material things likes to imagine that the dinosaurs could have existed forever. This, of course, is the plot of the movie *Jurassic Park*: humans bring back the dinosaurs. However, as Jeff Goldblum's character, the great scientist who is constantly warning about the problematic effects of such an experiment, points out, a world full of mammals and a world full of dinosaurs cannot really coexist.

The disappearance of the dinosaurs made way for the rise of mammals; it created a space for new possibilities. As death and resurrection are central tenets of Christianity, those who profess to follow Jesus should understand this better than anyone, and yet it's a truth easily forgotten. Nothing goes on forever, and while the end of one thing is sad, such an end portends a new beginning. This is both a key observation of ecosystems but also a central teaching of all spiritual traditions, and embracing this truth can help us appreciate our current crisis as one of new possibility and not simply despair.

The second important, and also hopeful, observation about a crisis in the created world is that when a problem arises in an ecosystem, so too does its cure.

Problem and Cure

Rudolph Steiner was a twentieth-century mystic and esoteric teacher whose work has led to numerous holistic activities including Waldorf education, biodynamic gardening, and a type of integrative medicine called anthroposophic healing.[3]

---

3. An excellent summary of anthroposophic medicine can be found at https://anthroposophicmedicine.org.

One of the central insights of this style of medical practice mirrors what we've been exploring about the climate crisis, namely, that illness is, in part, a manifestation of a spiritual problem. This is true both for individuals and also for societies. The disorder represents a spiritual imbalance or challenge that needs to be healed for the problem to resolve. On a social level, when we see a particular problem becoming epidemic, we seek to understand and address the spiritual condition that is one of the causes of the illness. In addition to this insight on the nature of illness itself, Steiner and other teachers noted, and this is one of the foundations of integrative and holistic medicine, that the cure for what ails us isn't far away or disconnected from the problem, but rather it appears simultaneously.

This co-arising of illness and cure is one manifestation of the teaching that God is always with us and tries to provide correctives when creation veers off course. Thus, today, as we notice a rise in anxiety, pain, and depression, and we understand these to be a manifestation of our alienated selves, we also see a rise in the desire for deep spiritual connection and grounding, for true nurture and an overcoming of disconnection. The ecological observation that natural systems are self-correcting confirms that problem and solution appear together in creation.

In the 1990s, my family and I lived in south central Vermont on a hilltop farm in a very small town. It's a beautiful place that lights up with color in the fall, and whose woods, hills, and valleys are lush with the wonderful ecosystem of hardwood deciduous trees. When we lived there, we spent a great deal of time in those woods without any concern for illness that might come from the mosquitos or flies that were, at times, annoying but nothing more.

Recently, my wife and I returned there to visit old friends, and we were stunned by one very significant change: the invasion of deer ticks and Lyme disease. This problem was completely unknown two decades ago, but now there is an epidemic so severe that some of our friends no longer walk in the woods, and the majority of people we talked to had either contracted Lyme disease or had a family member who had been ill. Of course, this invasion is the result of climate change; as the area has grown warmer, both the tick and the parasite can survive year round and become endemic.

At the same time, Vermont has another invader: Japanese knotweed. This plant, with its large leaves and small white flowers, loves to grow near rivers and can take over open river banks and rock beaches, weaving its shoots into enormous bush-like tangles. This infestation is also the result of climate change, and, not surprisingly, the average Vermonter hates this plant almost as much as they hate Lyme disease.

However, interestingly, if you ask an integrative medical practitioner what is the best herbal remedy for Lyme disease, the answer is Japanese knotweed. The problem and the cure have arrived in Vermont simultaneously, a phenomenon repeated throughout the world as we examine ecological problems. If there is an infestation of a particular bug, there is often a similar infestation of another bug who eats the first one. If there is a bacteria whose growth can throw a system out of balance, then a virus that controls that bacteria also appears. The same thing is true of spiritual challenges.

Since the mid-1950s, the mainstream church has been in steep decline in the United States and throughout the "developed world." People have been leaving organized Christianity in droves and the number of people who are identifying as "nones"—those with no religious affiliation—are increasing exponentially.[4] Of course, what people are leaving, in large mea-

---

4. Pew Research Center, "In U.S., Decline of Christianity

sure, is the alienated Christianity that we outlined earlier. Interestingly, this trend is occurring at exactly the same time as the dramatic rise in the alienated global social and economic systems that are churning out carbon and causing a rise in global temperature. And the Christianity that is one of the root causes of our climate crisis cannot be of help in dealing with the effects of the challenge it has helped to birth.

Fortunately, in sync with the rise of these problems, has been a massive surge in the interest in contemplative spirituality.[5] I first began my journey with contemplative practice four decades ago. In those days, contemplation was more for monks and nuns, hippies and freaks. You would never find a spiritual practice retreat in a mainline church or an article on mindfulness psychotherapy in a mainstream psychology journal. Such activities were either labeled outright evil, or, at best, flaky and irrelevant.

Now you cannot open a psychology or even mainstream medical journal without seeing an article or advertisement on mindfulness and prayer practices, and retreats are now understood to be of central importance to the life of faith within most church denominations. The interest in contemplation over these same four decades has been remarkable, and it also coincides with the rise of the climate crisis.

Contemplative practice and the spiritual teachings that accompany it are the opposite of an alienated faith. These activities, also called the "life of prayer" in the Christian tradition,

---

Continues at Rapid Pace: An update on America's changing religious landscape" (2019), www.pewforum.org.

5. For the purpose of this book the terms *contemplation*, *meditation*, *mindfulness*, *spiritual practice*, and *contemplative prayer* may be considered synonymous. There are some technical differences between them, but these are not relevant for our purposes.

center on a direct examination of our experience through the use of our minds and bodies, and they are designed to dissolve our ego state gently and lovingly, and not reinforce it. Thus, they do not draw us out of the world, separating ourselves from the rest of nature, but rather draw us into the world as we realize that the essence of our created core is one of interconnection and not alienation. In the rising interest in the spiritual life, we find the truth of the teaching that problem and cure appear together; humanity is being drawn toward these practices because we are instinctively yearning to heal our alienation, even while we cannot guarantee that such healing will stop planetary transformation (a topic discussed in the last section of the book). Our next chapter details the current movements in spirituality that summon the need for a set of practices grounded in our elemental reality.

3

The Rise of Embodied Spirituality

The spiritual nature of the climate crisis is one of *embodiment*. The earth is our physical home, and we are material beings in relationship with that home; thus, when one suffers, we all suffer together. Building on the observation of the previous chapter—that problems and solutions arise together—it is not surprising that, as the interest in spiritual practice has grown over these past decades, it has evolved in the direction of the body. What began as an interest in meditative practices that focus largely on mental activities that could be relegated to the realm of thought—silent meditation, chanting, repetitive prayers or mantras[1]—have increasingly developed into an interest in practices that have some significant involvement or focus on embodiment. For example, in many neighborhoods across America today you can find a yoga studio or class.

The climate crisis is also one of *trauma*, a term that describes the ramifications of the mistreatment of a material being. When we are abused in some way, when we are in a situation where we are unsafe, where our boundaries are violated, or where we are

---

1. In reality, these are not disembodied practices, but they are often thought of this way and can be practiced, incorrectly, without attention to our embodiment.

repeatedly scared, we experience a set of traumatic reactions. This is currently happening to the planet. The earth is being mistreated and responding with its own set of traumatic reactions. These too are embodied reactions and experiences, and just as people are gravitating toward embodied spiritual practice, so too are they gravitating toward the healing of trauma. These interrelated issues, the rise of embodied spirituality and the rise of an interest in trauma and healing, are key to understanding why a faith perspective and faith practices that tie us deeply to our elemental reality are now so vital.

Cursed Bodies

Several years ago, I was invited to lead a retreat in Louisiana. Although I'd been to New Orleans before, I had not spent much time in rest of the state, and my hosts and colleagues were determined to educate me on Louisiana culture. They delighted in sharing the oddest aspects of regular life in the state, laughing at my stunned reactions to things like the half-gallon sodas on sale at the local convenience store or the complete flight of white students from the public school system in an entire county. But what really floored me were the drive-through alcoholic beverage establishments.

These small shops, which looked like an ice-cream store, sell "daiquiris" in a cup. State law prohibits driving with an open container, but if you put a piece of tape across the top of the cup, the container is considered closed because you can't drink out of it, unless of course you have a straw. So the daiquiri comes with a piece of tape on the cup and a straw. But this isn't the best part.

The daiquiri isn't really a daiquiri because it doesn't contain any rum. Rather, it's made of flavored slushed ice and grain alcohol. This concoction is put into a Styrofoam cup, but this creates a problem because grain alcohol dissolves the Styrofoam (creating a viscous slime that is basically the same substance as napalm, the flammable chemical used in flame throwers and other weapons of war) and wears a hole in the cup. However, the stores have a simple solution to this problem: double cupping. It turns out that if you use two Styrofoam cups, you can finish your daiquiri before it melts the second cup. So in Louisiana, you have thousands of people driving around, drinking napalm, and enjoying themselves.

I wish I was making this story up, but I'm not. I was so stunned when one friend told me that I had to ask several other people, independently from each other, and it wasn't until the third or fourth person told me this was true that I finally had to believe them. And one of my first thoughts was: if a group of people will drink poison for fun, destroying their bodies as they do so, how can they possibly have any concern for the planet? This cultural artifact is just one example of what can only be described as a deep hatred of embodiment that is rampant in cultures that descend from European Christianity. Where does this hatred of embodiment come from? Sadly, from Christianity itself.

I wrote the book *Creating a Life with God*, which describes a wide array of prayer practices. The chapter "Body Prayer" begins:

> I begin this phase of our journey with one of the most difficult and controversial subjects in our faith: the body, our bodies. Why is this subject so difficult? Because for centuries the church has taken the position that the body is the seat of all evil. We have rejected, marginalized, even mutilated our bodies for the sake of our faith, and the collected historical weight of this rejection has lodged in our consciousness as a vague

underlying sense of shame and humiliation about our incarnated beings.[2]

This is also one of the cruelest paradoxes of the Christian faith because central to Christianity is the Incarnation of God: God, in Jesus, becomes embodied. God inhabits, and thus makes holy, embodiment; and yet, over time, the church has made the body bad. The reasons for this horrid twist of theology and practice are numerous, but the basic result is clear: our bodies have become cursed to us, and the pain of this legacy manifests in many ways, including the drive-through daiquiri stores. This disconnection from embodiment is another way to describe the alienation from our world and of our faith, because to deny our embodiment, to try and run from it, hide it, or ignore it, is an impossible task that can be accomplished only by the most painful twists of mind and denial of reality.[3] These are the effects of trauma, and it is to this subject that we now turn.

Humanity Has PTSD

Being human is traumatic. Spiritual teachings affirm this truth, although rather than using the word "trauma," they use terms like "fallen," "confused," "ignorance," and so on. The tribalism and the separate ego self that have been created by the appearance of the autonomous, aware human being not only alienates us from one another and the world, it also causes the behaviors that result in trauma. The wars, violence, manipulation, and cruelty in which humanity constantly engages, on top of the fundamental trauma of our delusion of separation

2. Daniel Wolpert, *Creating a Life with God: The Call of Ancient Prayer Practices* (Nashville, TN: Upper Room Books, 2003), 115.

3. I will return to this topic in greater detail in chapter 8.

from the rest of reality, result in the various states of being we call traumatic reactions.

Post-traumatic stress disorder (PTSD) is the most publicly recognizable diagnostic term in connection with the experience of trauma. This diagnosis describes one set of human responses to traumatic events.[4] These responses, which vary widely and broadly, include anxiety, frozen bodily states, seeing the world as our enemy, solidified negative ego patterns, and, in the most extreme manifestations, hallucinations, violent responses to ordinary stimuli, and the inability to perform basic life tasks.

Fifty years ago, this diagnosis, and the general awareness of trauma, was virtually unknown, even in professional psychological circles. Now, discussion of trauma is everywhere. At first, trauma studies and treatment focused on the purely mental manifestations of the traumatic reactions: anxiety, hypervigilance, or paranoia. However, as our awareness and understanding have grown, there is an increasing focus on the body and its role in holding and healing trauma and traumatic reactions.[5]

Thus, for those within the Christian faith, it is in our bodies that we find the intersection of the desire to heal and the problems created by a faith that tells us that our bodies are bad—a teaching that itself causes trauma. This very serious conundrum—the need to heal our bodies even as we are taught to hate them—is one of the things causing people to move away from Christianity toward more "indigenous" spiritualities that are considered to have a more positive view of embodiment.

---

4. For an overview of the diagnosis of trauma-related disorders, see American Psychiatric Association, *Diagnostic and Statistical Manual of Mental Disorders, 5th Edition: DSM-5* (Arlington, VA: American Psychiatric Publishing, 2013), 217–34.

5. For the best recent work on this topic, see Bessel van der Kolk, *The Body Keeps the Score: Brain, Mind, and Body in the Healing of Trauma* (New York: Penguin Books, 2015).

Problems and Possibilities

The desire for a healthier, embodied spirituality is a positive one, but it is also one that has a number of significant problems that must be addressed before we can make any movement toward a healthy nonalienated, elemental faith.

America, and the dominant American culture that is being spread worldwide, came into existence through the creation of what is now being called "whiteness." This term covers the entire spectrum of socio-economic and political structures that allowed for the establishment of slavery and the policy of Native American genocide that coincided with, and allowed for, the growth of this country. Those of us, myself included, who are able to identify as white are grafted into this legacy of racism and the ongoing privilege that such a system provides.[6]

For people who identify as white, one of the consequences of such a system is that it creates a "culture" of "whiteness" that in many ways is no culture at all. As people of color (POC) are wiped out and oppressed, causing massive pain and disruption, white people must, in order to survive and reap the fruits of such oppression, erase their backgrounds and cultures of origin in order to fit in with the generic "whiteness" of the dominant culture. As such, they leave their particular cultural backgrounds (Irish, Polish, Italian, etc.) to become "white." This is a soul-crushing activity, and one of the oppressive responses to this erasure is to appropriate cultural items from the very people who are being oppressed.[7] Examples of such appropri-

6. There are numerous recent and excellent books on white privilege. A less recent, but one of the best, is largely unknown because it was so far ahead of its time: Lillian Smith, *Killers of the Dream* (New York: W. W. Norton, 1978).

7. There are also many good works on this topic. For an excellent primer, see Maisha Z. Johnson, *What's Wrong with Cultural Appro-*

ation range from food choices, to the music industry, Native American sports logos, and white teens flashing "gang signs" at one another. These acts of appropriation are themselves part of the racist system of oppression.

Nowhere are these dual actions of the creation of a bland "white" culture and the process of cultural appropriation more apparent than in the sphere of religion and spirituality. Sadly, American Christianity was a full partner in the creation of the idea of whiteness, allowing the first laws that created the class of "white" people to be read in church every Sunday in the early seventeenth century.[8] Since then, the white American church has often propped up the racist structure of our country for centuries in its support of slavery, then segregation, and the genocide and cultural decimation of the Native American populations.

Less overtly, however, the white church has become part of the culture of whiteness through the promotion of a Christian faith that is completely disembodied from our current reality. The exclusive focus on individual salvation has created a faith that can easily ignore the oppressive society in which it is immersed. How else can you explain the criticism often heard in white churches in response to a sermon on social justice: "I don't mix faith and politics"? Here is another example of an alienated faith, this time maintaining the white status quo.

However, the response of those who identify as white and who wish to leave this type of faith and embrace a more embodied faith that connects to the natural world can be just as prob-

---

priation? These 9 Answers Reveal Its Harm, 2015, www.everyday feminism.com.

8. For an excellent summary account of the creation of whiteness in the United States, see Theodore W. Allen, "Summary of the Argument of *The Invention of the White Race* (Part One)," 1998, www.elegantbrain.com/edu4/classes/readings/race-allen.html.

lematic. The rise of New Age spirituality is often connected with the appropriation of Native American spiritualities and teachings, as well as the appropriation of a variety of Eastern religions. Thus, a white person participates in smudging or goes to a sweat lodge, thinking this is cool and indigenous without ever doing the work of dismantling racism or acknowledging their own privilege or complicity in a racist society.

This embracing of the "other's" spirituality without exploring one's own embodiment and history is just as alienated and disconnected, and continues the legacy of trauma, as the Christian faith that one abandoned. I am reminded of a story of an interaction between a Native American and a white biologist that occurred at a conference on water. The event was taking place in northwest Minnesota at a tribal college. This is a region with several Native American reservations, where the legacy of mistreatment of Native peoples lies not in the distant past but in very recent history. After the Native woman college president presented a paper on her people and the history of the area, the scientist spoke on the biological science of the region. She interrupted him and asked him, "Who are your people?" After a few stammering nonanswers, it became clear that he had no answer, or even a frame of reference. His people are "white Americans," which really is no people.

In order to arrive at an authentic embodied faith, one that faces the crises before us with justice, true equality, and healing, we must each dive deeply into our own story and faith history. If we are part of the class of oppressors, this journey involves deconstruction, confession, and repentance. If we are part of a predominantly oppressed group, it involves empowering our history and story and letting go of the process of erasure that accompanies oppression. In this task, we not only become liberated from the oppressive systems that bind us, and within which we participate, and experience healing from our traumatic existence but we also discover the root of every faith system that is grounded in the natural world.

From Ancient Desert to the Modern World

When people ask me who my people are, I begin with the most recent historical reality—that I am a Russian peasant, a Russian Jewish peasant. At some point, in the diaspora that occurred after the destruction of Jerusalem in 66 CE, my ancestors began moving north and east. My sense is that it took hundreds of years to make it to the area we now call western Russia, but eventually they became part of the small villages and communities that were a part of the czar's empire.

In the middle of the nineteenth century, the Russian army, made up of soldiers who probably considered themselves to be good Christians, began to destroy these villages and drive the Jewish population from their homes in a series of pogroms or persecutions. These were just another in a long series of traumatizing, anti-Semitic actions that are a part of European history and would reach their pinnacle with Nazi Germany and the Holocaust.[9] So, while destruction of Jewish homes wasn't unusual, these particular village burnings succeeded in driving my great grandparents from the place where their ancestors had settled, setting them, and the rest of the family, on a long journey to the United States, where they landed in New York shortly after 1900.

Two generations later, my nuclear family, nonreligious and

---

9. Tragically, the incidence of anti-Semitic hate crimes is once again on the rise throughout the world. This is yet another example of our ongoing tribal alienation.

culturally Jewish, ended up in Los Angeles, where I was born, a second-generation American. Growing up, our family story was deeply influenced by both the Holocaust and the creation of the State of Israel. This is a common reality for people of Jewish heritage raised in American during the 1960s and '70s. One of the challenging aspects of such a social location is that white American Jews tend to walk the line between identifying with the oppression that people of Jewish descent have faced over the years while also integrating into, and identifying with, the successes and privilege of white America. This Jewish community rightly receives criticism from communities of color that American Jews are on the front lines for social justice until it is inconvenient, and then they disappear into the world of white privilege.

The desire for both privilege and the incredible support for the State of Israel are two examples of how a legacy of trauma and oppression can become a legacy of being the oppressor. In psychological terms, people internalize the abuser and, through the process of unconscious acting out, try to protect themselves by abusing others. To this day, I am horrified that a people who died by the millions in "concentration camps" can create a country that herds people into "camps," as the Israelis have done with the Palestinian population. Yet I understand how this happens within an alienated and traumatized population.

Another aspect of the culturally and religiously Jewish reality in America is that there is a great identification with the ancient religious past, a past transmitted through the stories in the Hebrew Bible. Even in our nonreligious home, we regularly celebrated Passover and Hanukkah and told the ancient stories connected to these holidays: Moses and the exodus, and the Maccabean Revolt. These stories grounded our community in a deep continuity with the past and also told us something about a positive relationship between our people and the Divine. Thus, my history can be traced to this ancient experience in the desert regions we now call Israel/Palestine. What was the nature of such an experience?

Human history is long and complex, and our usual time horizon for what is considered "ancient" is inaccurate. For example, on a recent trip to Isle Royale in the middle of Lake Superior, I learned about a new theory of Neolithic peoples who used kayak-like boats to travel along the ancient glaciers from both the east and the west and populate what we call the Western Hemisphere long before a land bridge connected it with Russia. If humanity arose in Central Africa over a million years ago, there is a long time for humans to wander and inhabit parts of the earth before recorded history begins.

By the time the cult of YHWH (the four-letter Hebrew word for God) began east of Egypt, people had been coming and going from that part of the world for hundreds of thousands of years, a time frame that is challenging to comprehend. And for these millennia, people drew their understanding of reality from their direct experience of the rest of the natural world, for this was, of course, the entire substance of their existence. Without the trappings of the modern world that we take for granted, including the ability to use written language, people spent their entire lives observing, experimenting, and exploring the world around them and participating in a deep relationship with their external reality. Think of how one feels after a camping trip, and now multiply that by generations!

All aspects of one's life came directly from this natural relationship. Not only was it about food, shelter, healing, and community, it was also about Spirit. Long before written language appeared, groups of people across the globe related to their wider reality with song, story, ceremony, and mystical experience. Then, when written language arrived, these more ancient, embodied, nature-based practices were revealed in the stories that become scripture. The exodus story that I learned as a child is full of, and grounded in, these natural relationships. The space of the desert, the fire of the pillar with which God guides the people, the water of the Red Sea, the earth that yields manna and is the mountain that Moses climbs, and the air that holds the cloud that hides God, these elements are the basic substances used by God to engage the people on their journey to freedom.

Again and again in the ancient Hebrew Scripture, we see the connection between God and "nature" as God uses the natural world to communicate with humanity. We shouldn't be surprised by this intertwining of spirit and substance because, again, the natural world is all humanity had to "read." Furthermore, we see the same process unfolding in every indigenous group. Whether it is the indigenous populations in the Western Hemisphere, Australia, or across Asia or northern Europe, people developed a natural spirituality that understands human beings as one part of the great whole that is nature; and these spiritualities arise alongside the traumas of being human, and help and guide humanity to a place of goodness and healing. This truth reveals that any person, if they go back far enough in their history, originates from an indigenous background.

As I reflect on the span of time from my ancient roots to the villages of Russia and my family's experience in America, it seems as though humanity has taken a large detour from the deep, natural connection through the world of words and the manipulation of nature as an object and not a fellow subject. To develop the modern life we inhabit, we have needed, as a species, to distance ourselves from the material we manipulate. This is the alienation we have already noted and that we embrace when it benefits our ego selves but also hate when we are anxious and ill. Amid this ego struggle, the longing to connect deeply with the natural world remains. Studies consistently show that modern, urban people have their most profound experiences of God in nature. The threat of the climate crisis is a call to end this time of detour from a way of life that is disintegrated from the rest of the natural world.

The rise of embodied spiritualities and the desire to heal trauma are part of a movement toward our integration as a species and the recovery of the natural roots of spirituality and religion. It is the call of an elemental faith grounded in the contemplative experience and a relationship with wisdom. It is to this undertaking that we now turn.

4

Elemental Wisdom

The first three chapters explored the nature of our current climate crisis, revealing it as a deeply spiritual crisis that intersects with other issues of justice, social alienation, and trauma. Furthermore, in considering the underlying delusional nature of the individual ego, we can see how a solution to these problems, the healing balm that humanity needs, will come from a faith that works to bridge the divides between humanity and the rest of creation. We now turn to the particulars of such a faith, beginning with a discussion of the biblical wisdom tradition and then moving to an overview of the central component of this book, the Five Elements.

Ways of Wisdom

The biblical wisdom tradition is largely unknown to the average Christian. This is extremely unfortunate. While people have heard of Proverbs and may even know one or two, and while many people have had the famous "time for everything" speech from the book of Ecclesiastes read at a special service or listened to the song "Turn! Turn! Turn!," sung by The Byrds and based on that Scripture, the average person in the pew knows little about the wider teachings from which these passages are derived. I have had the experience of reading from the first nine chapters of Proverbs and being confronted by confused parishioners who wonder why I am calling Wisdom "she" and speaking as if Wisdom were a person.

This lack of knowledge stems from two main issues. First, the texts that comprise this particular part of the Bible personify Wisdom as a woman, perhaps even as the feminine face of God, and a patriarchal faith would rather ignore such teachings. This is not dissimilar to churches ignoring that the first person to proclaim the resurrection was a woman when they wish to argue against woman pastors and priests. Second, the wisdom tradition is profoundly experiential and contemplative and not doctrinal. Thus, it is of limited use (other than to try and turn individual proverbs into commandments) to a faith based on doctrine, which certainly defines most of church history. This claim finds support as we see that the greatest adherents and followers of the wisdom tradition lie within monastic communities; for they are seeking a way of living and being more than a set of doctrines to memorize and give intellectual assent to.

Yet, it is exactly for these same two reasons that the wisdom tradition is so helpful in our current time: in it we have support for balancing a highly patriarchal faith with other gendered perspectives, and we need resources that point us toward experience and not just doctrine. In our time of climate crisis, there is now a third reason for using the wisdom tradition: its connection to the natural world and creation, and the continuation of life. Proverbs 8:22–31 describes how Wisdom was the first of God's creations and that after she was brought forth, she and God created the universe, rejoicing and delighting (vv. 30–31)

in each other and in their work, the inhabited world. Then once
the creation is established, Wisdom develops her "ways," which
are the ways of goodness and life: "Her ways are ways of pleas-
antness, and all her paths are peace" (Proverbs 3:17).

Yet in order to access Wisdom one must have a relationship
with her, her teachings, and these paths. This is a description of
the spiritual life, the life of contemplation. The creation of such
a life—a life lived in community with others and established by
Wisdom—is outlined in beautiful allegorical form in Proverbs
9:1–6. Here, Wisdom creates a space where people are invited to
a banquet that feeds them not only literally but also spiritually.

Christian theologians have noted in this passage a presaging
of the communion ritual, which is also an invitation to spiritual
feeding. Whether or not this particular association is true, there
is no question that the focus of such a banquet is not just physical nourishment, for the last verse reveals the real purpose of
the invitation—to "leave simpleness, and live, and walk in the
way of insight" (Proverbs 9:6). Through the many chapters that
follow this invitation, it is revealed that the way of insight is a
life that requires attention to our actions, our relationships, the
choices that we make both internally and externally, in relation
to ourselves and others. We will explore these themes in greater
depth in the chapters that follow, for now what is important is
the realization that the wisdom tradition speaks to us of a nonalienated, awakened faith that draws us into right relationship
with creation.

The existence of this tradition of wisdom is not unique to
the Hebrew Bible. There are many other wisdom traditions in
the world. Of course this makes sense. If Wisdom is indeed primordial, as Proverbs 8 describes, and if Wisdom's work is seen
in nature and in humanity, in both the being and the act of
creation, then it is not surprising that Wisdom is found every-

where.[1] As humans facing an evolving world in crisis, we must
find Wisdom wherever she resides, and there is a long history
of Christianity adopting and engaging teachings, philosophies,
and practices that help develop the faith across time and culture. As noted in the introduction, there is hardly an aspect of
modern Christian worship and practice that doesn't derive from
some "non-Christian" source.

Furthermore, in the previous chapter, we discussed negative
cultural appropriation and so it is important to ask, What is
the difference between learning from, and using positively, an
aspect of another culture versus a cultural appropriation that is
oppressive? There is no clear answer to this question, but there
are several valuable guidelines. First, negative cultural appropriation occurs within the context of oppression. If, as a white
man in America, I do not acknowledge my privilege and the
racist society to which I belong and commit to a practice of anti-
racism, then any "borrowing" from other cultures usually ends
up being appropriation.

Second, as we noted earlier, cultural appropriation often
occurs when one is trying to avoid one's own background or fill
the "culture" void—in the case of America, by whiteness. One
of my Tibetan teachers, Tarthang Tulku, was adamant when
he conveyed Buddhist teachings to the West that Americans
not become Buddhists per se but rather that they use the Buddhist teachings to go deeply into their own backgrounds and
traditions. If the result of this exploration was an authentically
Western Buddhism, that was one thing, but he encouraged his
students to first understand where they came from.

Finally, a negative cultural appropriation is accompanied by
a lack of acknowledgment of the culture of origin and a deval-

---

1. See the introduction for a brief discussion on Christianity's
challenging relationship to "natural theology."

uation of the persons from whom you are appropriating. For example, we hear white people making numerous racist and derogatory remarks about Native Americans while at the same time insisting that they are "honoring" these peoples by using their sports logos. Clearly, there are a variety of complex dynamics at play when cultures interact; thus it is of great importance to be aware of these issues and name these challenges as we engage in cross-cultural work.

With these challenges in mind, I now turn to a set of wisdom teachings from the regions of Tibet and China. These teachings came to the West in the second half of the twentieth century and were developed in several centers in both the United States and Europe. At the Naropa University, they developed as a set of practices called Maitri (meaning loving kindness) Space Awareness Practice.[2] In Scotland, they were used to create a therapeutic system called Tara Rokpa.[3] While in California, they were an integral part of Tarthang Tulku's work at the Nyingma Institute and the Odyian Retreat Center.

FIVE WISDOM TEACHINGS

Human cultures have recognized that the material world, in its diversity and complexity, is built from simple, elemental building blocks. Today, the scientific communities of the world, those that owe their culture to the scientific tradition of modernity, have identified 118 of these elements, although only 92 of these occur naturally on earth.[4]

---

2. Irini Rockwell, *The Five Wisdom Energies: A Buddhist Way of Understanding Personalities, Emotions, and Relationships* (Boulder, CO: Shambhala, 2002).

3. See www.tararokpa.org for detailed information on this technique.

4. See the Western periodic table of the elements.

Ancient China also developed an elemental tradition, but in this case there were only five elements: wood, fire, earth, metal, and water.[5] As with our modern elements, these are understood to be the building blocks of the entire natural world. However, unlike modern elemental theory, the Chinese elements are not only material in nature but also "energetic," what we might call spiritual. Thus the elements are connected to Qi, the basic energetic life force, or spirit; and the combination of elements not only provides substance to everything in the universe, but they also provide the energy needed for life and health. Elemental theory as it developed was, therefore, not only part of material science, but it also became an essential component of Chinese medicine, where the balance of the elements and their energetic qualities determined health or illness. In health, the elements are balanced and available in sufficient quantity. An imbalance in the elements, however, due to an excess or insufficiency, results in illness.[6]

The Chinese Five Element theory and the disciplines that drew from this theory, including traditional Chinese medicine and a wide variety of mind/body practices for health and spirituality, flourished within ancient China and spread to regions throughout Asia. As the theory encountered other cultures, some of the elemental designations were changed and adapted to different regions. In Tibet, the five elements were designated air, earth, water, fire, and space. Given the geography and topology of Tibet, it is possible to imagine how air and space may

---

5. An excellent summary of the Chinese Five Element theory can be found at www.shen-nong.com.

6. The description of illness formation in traditional Chinese medicine is, of course, far more complex than simple imbalance, but this is one of the central problems that leads to illness.

have seemed more elemental to Tibetan culture than wood and metal.

From approximately 400 BCE to 800 CE, Buddhism was also spreading throughout Asia, moving north and east from India, where it encountered and mixed with the variety of Five Element theories. This interaction created new types of teachings related to wisdom and the natural world. When Buddhism arrived in Tibet, it developed their elemental approach, which was integrated into Buddhist teachings to create the Five Wisdom understanding of reality.

As with the earlier Chinese system, the Tibetan Five Elements are not just material elements; rather, they are the energetic building blocks of everything material, psychological, and spiritual. Thus, each element is not inert but "alive" with wisdom; each element is considered to have a self-existing intelligence. In Christian terms, each element is like an attribute of God, or an aspect or manifestation of God.[7]

These elements and their wisdom quality infuse everything in creation, from rocks to people to organizations. They are associated with a particular color, a season (or in the case of space, all the seasons), as well as foods, natural environments, styles of dress and decoration, as well as varying aspects of culture.

Because the elements are everywhere, they are often described as inhabiting space, or being spacious. Because space is included as one of the elements, this can be confusing, but, when referring to the elements as a whole, space simply means three dimensional space—the space we inhabit. This description is meant to help us draw our awareness to the created reality. The elemental energy fills this space, fills our beings, and fills our minds. It isn't static or separate from us for we exist within the elemental reality. This view is similar to biblical wisdom, who is beside

---

7. This idea will be discussed further in the chapters that follow.

God in every creative act and meets people in every thought.[8] She also inhabits the space within which we exist.

In order to understand how the Five Wisdoms interact with our contemplative life and practice and our experience of being human, we must return to the nature of our human-ego experience understood through the lens of contemplative psychology.

WISDOM AND NEUROSIS

As we noted in chapter 2, the process of ego formation creates our experience of a separate self. This isn't a bad thing per se, for without it, we couldn't function in the world; with the ability to be autonomous and manipulate reality, however, comes the alienation and trauma of our human existence.

How does our mind create this separate self?[9] From the moment of infancy, our jobs as newborn humans is to make sense of the world. Anyone who's been around a baby knows that intense baby-staring-into-space-because-I'm-so-overwhelmed look. At this early stage of our development, we are busy taking in billions of bits of information and sorting them into intelligible patterns. At the most basic level of our data management system, each piece of information goes into one of three categories: like, dislike, or ignore. Amazingly, the "ignore" category comprises about 95 percent of our experienced reality. If you don't believe me, do a small experiment to prove it: next time you drive somewhere,

---

8. Wisdom of Solomon 6:16.

9. There are many outstanding works on contemplative psychology. Two excellent examples are, first, from the Buddhist perspective, Tarthang Tulku, *Time, Space, and Knowledge: A New Vision of Reality* (Berkeley, CA: Dharma Publishing, 1977); and from the Christian perspective, Martin Laird, *An Ocean of Light: Contemplation, Transformation, and Liberation* (Oxford: Oxford University Press, 2019).

after you arrive, try remembering the make, model, and color of every car you passed on the road. Of course, this is impossible. Even though this information reached your brain, it was automatically ignored because it was deemed irrelevant; and that's the point of this "ignore" category. If we tried to remember and process every piece of information that wandered into our brain via our nervous system, we would be completely overwhelmed and couldn't function. The world is just too big.

Following this first basic sorting gateway, we use the remaining small amount of information in the "like" and "dislike" categories to construct our particular version of reality. We then project this created world, what is called conceptual reality, onto the real world in order to be equipped to function as autonomous humans. Our ego is created, and we are at the center of the world as we know it. Unfortunately, we are unaware of this process, and we believe that we are engaging the world as it is, not the world as we have formed it. This is the basic delusional nature of our separate selves, and it is the cause of the alienation we experience. One image of our ego state that I've often used when teaching is a human stick figure inside a bubble. The bubble is our invisible world projection. The earth is populated by billions of people, each in their own bubble, bumping into one another, thinking they share the same world, and wondering why there is constant confusion, conflict, and misunderstanding. Spiritual teachings have referred to this state by several names, original sin in Christianity, but in the contemplative Buddhist world, this is our neurotic mind.

The Book of Proverbs uses the term "fool" to describe our ego selves. This term is problematic because, after centuries of judgmental religious practice, it carries a perspective that is not particularly compassionate. Perhaps this term is beyond redemption, and, if it feels unhelpful to you, that's fine. Here we can see the hard truth that every teaching, no matter how wise, has aspects that are not helpful and need to be amended and reformed. Jesus himself frequently did this in relation to the religion of his times, often breaking "the law" or rejecting parts of Scripture in order to reveal a more helpful teaching. For our purposes, note that the biblical wisdom tradition contains within it an understanding of the ego self similar to the Buddhist tradition.

Contemplative practice, which can be defined as the direct examination of reality using the tool of our awareness, seeks to slowly dissolve the bubble and lead us out into the real world beyond our projections. It does this by allowing the speed of our minds, which is the tool that maintains our view of reality much like an old movie creates a moving picture out of stills by moving them very quickly, to relax and slow down. This opening is aided by the compassion and loving kindness that spontaneously arise as a result of contemplative practice that, in turn, allows us to develop great care for ourselves and others. If we are curious and friendly toward our experience, we see ourselves and the world more clearly; we can peek out into the world through our bubble, much like a shy animal coming out from its home into the field or forest.

The spiritual life is often described as the life of nonduality. Sometimes this term can seem overly esoteric, strange, or even absurd because it may imply that there is no difference between anything. But it doesn't have to be any of these abstract ideas; rather it simply refers to the notion that, as we sit, examining the world directly, we have an attitude of compassion toward our experiences, which allows great awareness to arise. This relaxation and awareness slowly erodes the habitual patterns of our sorting system, and we now allow more of the information about the world through our "ignoring" function and the

judgmental quality of our "like" and "dislike" filters. We see
things as they really are, and we experience a deep connection
with the rest of reality. Again, every spiritual tradition has terms
for this experience. In Buddhism, this is the experience of wisdom or Enlightenment, and in Christianity it is Union with
God or the Way of Wisdom.

While these processes may sound abstract, they are not; and
we experience the movement from a more neurotic state to a wisdom state naturally. For example, we've all had the experience
of a misunderstanding with a friend or loved one. We are sure
that we know what is going on, and we are very distressed about
what's happening. Often, we assume the worst about the other
person, their feelings, their intentions, and their actions. When
we are in the midst of the argument, we are both trapped within
the solidity of our separate bubbles, and it feels very claustrophobic and painful. Then, somehow, we are able to converse in
an open way. We learn that they aren't thinking or feeling any of
the things we assumed, or they acted with very different motiva-
tions than we ascribed to them. When this happens, we can feel
the entire situation open, and we once again experience connection with our friend. This is the moment when the bubbles
have, temporarily, popped and we are no longer alienated and
alone. This movement from neurosis to wisdom is a normal part
of our experience, and contemplative practice helps us to move
toward wisdom more frequently and with greater reliability as
we engage the world. So how does this process connect to the
Five Wisdoms and Elements?

Our Energetic Experience

The world that our ego self is trying to comprehend and manipulate is made up of complex combinations of the Five Elements.
This includes the world outside of our selves but also inside of

our selves. We are not separate from "nature" and the elemental world but are part of it; we exist in space. Thus, the energy and the intelligence of these elements are moving in and around us at every moment. Christians affirm this in acknowledging that God is everywhere and in everything. Even our individual intelligence is made up of a combination of elemental energy and wisdom.

Therefore, as our ego forms the habits of our separate mind and identity, we are always in relationship with this elemental reality, and our relationship with this reality is either neurotic or wise. This action and power of our ego is determined by many things, including the traumas we've experienced; our traumatic reactions become part of our ego habits as we attempt to defend ourselves from the world that has caused us harm. When our ego is either trying to cling to the elemental wisdom, or when it feels alienated from such wisdom, we experience a neurotic relationship with that particular energy. In contrast, when we are in an open state, a state where we align with wisdom, we experience a wise relationship with that particular energy.

As with any contemplative practice, elemental practice helps us move freely from the neurotic to the wisdom experience, and the teachings associated with these practices help us to understand the nature of each element and describe the experience of both the wisdom and the neurotic relationship to the element. The next five chapters examine each element in detail, including its wisdom nature and also our neurotic experience. This examination will help us move from our alienated state into the ways of wisdom, ways that draw us closer to God and help us in our relationships with the created world.

5

The Wisdom of Space:
A Loving Container

Wisdom has built her house, she has set up her seven pillars.
—Proverbs 9:1

Northwest Minnesota, where my family and I lived for many years and which is still the location of the MICAH (Minnesota Institute of Contemplation and Healing) Retreat Center, is a vast place. The plains of the Red River Valley are almost completely flat and devoid of trees, except along the riverbeds, and the sky stretches for miles.

The visible distances are so great that they are deceiving, because you cannot see that far in many other places. When making a left turn on a country road at night, it is instinctual to stop when you see the headlights of an oncoming vehicle. And you wait, and wait, only to realize that the approaching car is miles away and that it is safe to turn. Once I was sitting on the deck of a restaurant watching a large thundercloud grow. It seemed nearby. Curious as to the storm's location, I looked at the radar and found that it was sixty miles in the distance.

These endless spaces make large buildings appear tiny, and if you are walking, you may find yourself never reaching that clump of trees that you thought was just "down the road" but is actually ten miles away. The space also produces visual displays in the sky that are rarely found elsewhere. Clouds that can be dozens of miles long form into huge sky creatures, and sunsets are a spectacular display of infinite shades of reds, pinks, purples, blues, and greens. In the winter, the ice crystals in the air create fantastic arcs of light and rainbows around the sun that arch across dozens of miles of the heavenly dome. At night, the Milky Way is visible in all its splendor, billons of stars dotting the night sky, or, if the moon is full, the lens of the heavens reflects so much light that you can see in color even at night.

Such a landscape manifests, as its primary element, the first of the Five Elements—space.

An Unusual Element

Space is not what most people would think of as an "element," which we generally associate with something tangible, solid, material; space is the opposite of these things. Yet, as the Five Element theory moved from China to Tibet, with its vast plateaus and huge mountains, the Chinese element metal became the Tibetan element space. This element is the element of container; it is the element that holds all the elements, for without a container, no form is possible. Not surprisingly, the color of space is white—the color comprised of every color—and space is associated not with one season but with the entire calendar year.

In the creation story in Genesis 1, we hear that, after God creates light, God makes a space between the waters with the firmament. This is the environment within which the earth, and then life, appears. Without this space, life isn't possible, yet because space is so ubiquitous and obvious in our experience, we often take it for granted.

Yet every day we reap the benefits of being three dimensional. Can you imagine life as a line—two dimensionality—or
a point—one dimensionality? It wouldn't be much fun. Three
dimensionality is what allows the world to have form and our
bodies to exist. While these statements may seem obvious, we
rarely take time to examine the nature of this three-dimensional
reality we inhabit. We lack an awareness of this space, without
which we would be nothing.

Sometimes, however, we do notice space. When we enter an
amazing building, hike to a spectacular view or grove of trees,
or enter a place where people have sat in prayer or meditation
for centuries, we are taken by the nature of the space itself. This
is true even if we are focused on the things in the space. I recall
the many holy spaces I have been to in my life: churches, cathedrals, caves that were the site of ancient rituals, mountain tops,
deserts, and temples. These spaces have an electric presence that
does not simply come from the material objects in the space.

This is because the container we inhabit isn't an inert, blank
space, but, rather, it has properties, qualities, an essential nature
that allows the other elements to function. Peter Stevens's fas-
cinating work *Patterns in Nature* explores the qualities of space,
noting that certain patterns, such as hexagons, spirals, and other
geometric shapes, repeat throughout the animate and inanimate
world. In this scientific exploration of space, Stevens confirms
the ancient wisdom that space engages in a relationship with the
matter inhabiting space.[1]

Yet the activity of elemental space extends beyond the material. Space is also the container for spiritual reality. My experience in these holy spaces doesn't merely derive from the aspects
of space that allow molecules to arrange themselves such that

---

1. Peter S. Stevens, *Patterns in Nature* (New York: Little Brown,
1974).

the proteins in my body can perform their assigned functions. Rather, space is also a holder of wisdom, and this active spaciousness is the element that the ancient Tibetans, the ancient Hebrews, and all ancient peoples realized was a vital part of our elemental reality.

THE WISDOM OF SPACE

In the biblical world, the primary image of space is the wilderness. This derives directly from people's experience of the desert, which, like northwest Minnesota, is an environment whose foundational element is space. In the vast quiet of a desert landscape, one can feel the power of space itself, and some of the most significant spiritual encounters of the Bible occur within this desert setting. Whether it is the story of the Israelites in the wilderness or Jesus or Elijah in the wilderness, going into the element of vast space allows for a powerful spiritual encounter with God, with oneself, and with the cosmic forces at work in the universe. Through these stories, we can see mirrored the teachings from the Five Element theory that the wisdom quality of the element space is the wisdom of enlightenment.

In the previous chapter, we noted how each element is not simply physical but also has spiritual and psychological qualities; they are nonmaterial "energies," nonmaterial intelligence. Buddhism is a nontheistic—without God—religion, and so it would not call this intelligence God but rather enlightened mind. In a theistic—with God—religion like Christianity, we would use the term God to describe this nonmaterial intelligence and would say that the wisdom of the elements is the wisdom of the divine being.

In the element of space, we see the totality of divine wisdom. Consequently, in biblical stories, people encounter God in the desert. Faced with the element of space, Moses and the prophets are gifted with a divine encounter. Jesus, as the incarnation of the Divine, engages in a spiritual encounter with the fallen forces of the universe within the element of space and emerges with a great sense of clarity about his work and ministry. The spiritual qualities of the element of space derive from the vastness of wisdom.

Just as a desert landscape can absorb the sound of your voice no matter how loud you yell, whether the sound is muffled by vast sands or dissipates in echoes down a canyon, so too the element of space can accommodate everything and anything. Here, there is a great openness to whatever arises in one's heart and mind. No thought, no feeling is blocked out or removed; everything is present just as it is.

In Proverbs 9, Wisdom builds her house, her space, her container, and then invites everyone from the town to come and join her. No one is excluded; everyone is welcome. This theme is repeated in the New Testament in the story of the great banquet (Luke 14:15–24). When the ruler finds that the invited friends have not come to his feast, to the "container" he has set for them, he tells his servants to go out and round up anyone they can find and bring them to the meal. In both scriptural accounts, there is an invitation into spaciousness. This spaciousness is so vast, open, and powerful that the tradition claims that no one shall see the face of God and live, as our created minds would be overwhelmed by an encounter with the vastness of God's mind. Yet, the Christian contemplative tradition, which invites us into the spaciousness of God, flips this warning as the community prays that its members shall see the face of God and live.

The wisdom of space is the wisdom of equanimity, of a vast stillness and calm. Any neurosis and disturbance of heart and mind can be met with a peaceful compassion that is loving and healing. As Christianity began to develop, thousands of seekers went into the deserts of Egypt, Syria, and Palestine desiring a divine encounter. Known as the desert mothers and fathers, these contemplatives entered the wilderness to find God. One of the most famous of these hermits was St. Anthony of the Desert, who is said to have lived in caves meditating and praying for ninety years. During this time in vast space, Anthony encountered the demons of his mind, of the world, as well as the Spirit of God. Stories are told of students who would come to Anthony for advice only to hear him being thrown about his cave by these spirits! Over the years, as Anthony emerged from these experiences, it was said that he possessed a palpable expansive equanimity and was continually sought out for his wisdom and teachings. His mind had taken on many of the qualities of the wisdom of space.

In these stories, we are reminded of one of most important aspects of the teachings of the Five Wisdoms. These elements are not just outside of us, around us in the world, but they are also inside us; we are made of the elements. Our ego self, which is constantly engaged in projection and is fascinated by the outside world and the projects of our lives, tends to focus on the external nature of the elemental world, This is why we experience alienation in our lives. We are cut off both from ourselves and, despite our fascination, the true outside world. The Five Wisdom teachings understand that, from an elemental perspective, there is no "inside" and "outside" but rather only reality itself. As we enter the wisdom of space, we can experience this vast openness around us but also within us. We do not need to be afraid of our thoughts and feelings or judge one as good and one as bad. All are welcome; there is room for all at wisdom's table. This is the essence of compassion and loving kindness.

The wisdom of space is thus extremely nondualistic, a theme alluded to earlier in relation to contemplative practice as a whole. Just as we hear that God has created everything (see Isaiah 45:7), so too the wisdom of space resists judging between "this" and "that." Our ego self is constantly trying to pick sides, to start an argument over right and wrong, good or bad. Anyone who has engaged social media can see this process instantly. Today, we hear about people's "silos," the affinity groups we join online within which we exercise a tyrannical purity of thought and feeling and lob the weapons of words and ideas toward the other silos, which are, of course, wrong and bad. The wisdom of space is the container that holds all the silos, allowing them to exist or not exist, rise and fall, while remaining silent, open, accepting. This wisdom invites us out of our little worlds into the vast world of God. Yet, this great space is a threat to our ego selves, and it is from such a threat that the neurotic aspects of the energy of space arise.

The Neurotic Experience of Space

Despite the incredible beauty and wonder of the northern plains, it is often described as boring or even ugly. "It's just flat; there's nothing to see here," is often heard. We have a hard time convincing people to come to our retreat center because folks think it's in a vast, dull, middle-of-nowhere place that isn't worth the trip. These comments and attitudes reveal the neurotic human response to the space element: ignoring reality.

Remember that when we talk about the neurotic experience of an element we aren't saying that the element itself has some neurotic qualities. This would be the same as saying that God has neurotic qualities. Wisdom is always the same. She is radiant and beautiful and always ready to greet us. The foolishness, the neurosis that arises in our interaction with ourselves and the world, comes not from wisdom but rather from our relationship with ourselves and the world. There are two primary ways that our ego, our bubble person, responds to the wisdom of an element, and often they are combined or we move from one to another.

The first is that we experience the wisdom of the element as something separate from ourselves that we lack or we actively reject. In this stance, we place ourselves outside of wisdom, and from here one of two things can happen. Either we experience this lack as a painful diminishment of self, the essence of low self-esteem, or we respond to this separateness as if we are a god and have our own unique wisdom to rely on. Both experiences are frequently mentioned in the book of Proverbs, where the fool elevates their own counsel or thoughts, rejecting the wisdom that is offered from God, and either becoming puffed up and wicked, or poor and destitute, lacking everything. In the Buddhist tradition, this experience of separation is described as understanding oneself to be self-reliant and standing apart from everything and everyone.

The second ego style appears when the ego tries to appropriate wisdom for itself. Here we aren't standing apart from the wisdom of the element but are trying to possess it and make it into an ego project. This approach is a manifestation of the primary narcissism of the ego self. The story of the Tower of Babel is an allegory of this state of being: humans believe that they can build a tower to God and take over heaven. That we can possess wisdom is the delusion under which the ego labors.

Either of these relationships with wisdom, or some combination of both, results in the neurotic experience of each element; and as we describe each of the elements, we will see these two dynamics play out again and again. This microcosm of our individual relationship with elemental wisdom is the foundation for our social, global relationship with wisdom and thus is the foundation of the crises we are currently facing. On a global level, we continue to believe that we are separate from the wisdom of the elements and can ignore or control that wisdom. We are gradually seeing the foolishness of this approach.

The neurotic experience of space, of a wisdom of vast lovingness and infinite accommodation, is thus an experience of ignorance or god-like absorption. When the ego tries to ignore the spaciousness, taking the stance of being separate from wisdom, it has an experience that is dull, limited, "spaced-out," or in denial. In the descriptions of the elemental neurotic states, Buddhist teachings speak of the different "realms" that the ego inhabits as it responds to each wisdom. One realm is the animal realm, depicted by an image of a pig with its head in the mud. This is the neurotic experience of space. Our heads are down; we are completely unaware; nothing penetrates our consciousness.

Serving as a pastor in northwest Minnesota, I would often use pictures I took of the sunsets as part of audiovisual presentations in worship. On multiple occasions, people would ask in wonder where these beautiful images of sunsets came from. I would share that I took them in the high school parking lot, or just outside of town, and people were amazed. I would encourage them to look up at the sky. Soon people began sending me messages about the beauty of the sky they were observing. In the face of vast space, a normal response of the human ego is to feel small and insignificant, and so we, literally and figuratively, put our heads down and ignore more and more of our experience. This cuts us off from the wisdom of space, which invites us to share in the vastness of God. "Don't bother me with facts." "Let's just forget about it." "Don't worry it will go away; climate changes all the time." These comments manifest the neurosis of space.

When the ego tries to own spacious wisdom, the ignorance remains; yet now the ego thinks that the space is theirs. This is the megalomaniac, who tries to conquer everything, own everything, and never listens to anyone or allows for any input or reflection. As an institution, Christianity, as it aligned with European kings to promote the doctrine of discovery,[2] was embracing this neurotic relationship with space: *the space is ours, and we will own it, and take it over no matter who or what stands in our way, for we are right and righteous.* The biblical kings, who refuse to listen to the Law and instead try to impose their own will, creating an unjust kingdom, also show an ego-driven approach to space.

In both neurotic experiences, the openness of space is destroyed and frozen. We feel claustrophobic or numb. This is the experience of silent isolation or a clueless imperialism. Recently, I saw a super yacht that was owned by a Russian billionaire who has made his fortune on coal and other mining as well as logging. This boat is bigger than I ever could have imagined. It's almost the size of a large cruise ship. Way up on one of the decks was a small child's playground set. I imagined the owner's few children playing there, parents sitting nearby. That vast space was theirs; and yet, they are completely alone, cut off and alienated from the world even as they make decisions that are harming billions of people, and all the while thinking they were wise but really being the biggest fools of all.

From Ignorance to Openness

The wisdom traditions of the world and the contemplative path are fundamentally optimistic in that we are taught that we can wake up at any moment, for wisdom is always there. As we come to understand both the neurotic and the wise aspects of the

---

2. For an excellent indigenous discussion and description, see www.doctrineofdiscovery.org.

elemental experience, we see the manifestations of both experiences everywhere, and we train our minds to move from the neurotic stance to the enlightened, or wise, relationship.

A neurotic relationship to space is present all around us—in the denial of the substance abuser, the climate change denier, and those who refuse to listen to anyone who doesn't agree with them. Social constructions such as private property and national boundaries, which divide an earth that isn't owned by any of its creatures but whose bounty should be available to everyone, also manifest an ego-driven relationship to space.

In our own lives, we can see how we shrink from greater spaciousness by denying our worth, our value, our very bodies. In patriarchal social structures, women are taught not to take up space, a message so ubiquitous that there are even clothes sizes less than zero. In racist social spaces, those who are of the oppressed groups are also taught not to hold space and what spaces they can live in or occupy. Police practices, banking practices known as redlining, and, the most blatant example, detainment camps are designed to limit space for these oppressed groups of people.

Yet wisdom invites us to overcome these personal and social habits and move toward greater, more open, spaciousness. The most basic and powerful way to do the Five Element practice is to spend time with the particular element, noticing how our mind and body respond and gently training our awareness toward the wisdom qualities that emerge naturally as we engage the element.

When I am in northwest Minnesota, one of my favorite practices is to take long bike rides in the countryside, especially at sunset. I ride slowly, head up, watching and experiencing the vast space around me. Frequently I stop to photograph the spectacular clouds and distant vanishing points. These activities bring me into direct and sustained contact with space. I can feel the limitlessness within me and around me, and my mind and body expands, becoming a part of the incredible environment of this planet. As this experience unfolds, it comes with a great peace and a sense of endless acceptance. This is the equanimity of space that arises spontaneously as we train our awareness toward this element.

We noted earlier that the elemental system has a medicinal aspect and that each element connects primarily with an organ system, or meridian, in the body. The main organ system for space is the lungs. While this may seem odd, since the air element intuitively fits the lungs, they are the place where inner space and outer space are most connected. As our lungs expand, our inner space literally increases and we bring the spaciousness of the world into us.

It is perhaps not surprising that as our world feels smaller or we become more anxious, less open, afraid, and alone, we also stop breathing. I spend significant time in my individual healing practice reminding people to breath and teaching simple breathing techniques like 4-7-8 breathing.[3] This can make us aware of our breath, and as we do, we will not only notice when we do not breathe, cutting ourselves off from space, but we can also avail ourselves of the peace and relaxation of spaciousness by simply placing our hand on our abdomen and breathing deeply.

We can also practice noticing space in our work, our relationships, and the choices we make about our time and resources. When we are with others, do we take up much space or never use the space? How do we feel in the midst of spaciousness, or when we are the focus of the space? If we are tense and awkward, can we practice allowing ourselves to be present within a space?

---

3. The technique is very simple: breathe in for a count of 4, hold your breath for a count of 7, breath out for a count of 8. Repeat three times. Google 4-7-8 breathing for many references.

If we are working on healing from trauma, we can note when we are safe in space. One exercise I frequently prescribe is that people walk around their living space noting that they are safe and can occupy the space without worry.[4]

Spending time noticing and engaging the element of space is deeply healing, energizing, and empowering. It is not surprising that social justice movements encourage and discuss the need for the oppressed to claim their space in the world. We are embodied, three dimensional beings, who are given the space within which we are called to extend the love that is shown us as created beings. The Incarnation is the advent of God inhabiting this three-dimensional world for the purpose of manifesting wisdom. As Buddhists say, you cannot be Enlightened without a mind, and a mind requires space.

Yet this spaciousness is just the beginning of our elemental journey. It is the vast container; and now that it's in place, we can examine the elements that use this container for their endless play, starting with the element of water.

---

4. Of course this recommendation assumes that the person is in fact safe in their home and not in an ongoing abusive situation.

6

The Wisdom of Water: Clarity

And a wind (Spirit) from God swept over the face of the waters.

—Genesis 1:2b

Water is an amazing, almost magical substance. Chemically, this "magic" arises from its structure, which allows water to be the container for life. The three atoms of the water molecule—two atoms of hydrogen and one of oxygen—form a triangular shape. The two hydrogens each occupy a corner of the triangle while the oxygen atom sits with two of its electrons exposed to the rest of the world.

Because of this spatial arrangement, water is able to interact with itself and other molecules in a loose but firm lattice using what are called hydrogen bonds. These weak chemical bonds allow water to exist in all three states of matter—solid, liquid, and gas—within the very narrow temperature range of earth, an extremely rare occurrence for a compound, and also allow water to be a holding substance for large molecules. This is because hydrogen bonds don't create new substances but rather act like the strings of a puppet, holding and guiding these larger molecules as they interact and engage in the processes essential for life.

roteins surrounded by water are able to perform their processes. Similarly, DNA and RNA, the genetic ...... f life, are able to zip and unzip as they are read by the cellular structures that produce the proteins that define a given organism. Water also allows fats and carbohydrates to arrange themselves so that cells form and can provide the energy an organism needs to live. None of these activities would be possible without water; and it is no surprise that when scientists look into space, searching for planets that might contain life, they ask, Is there water on this planet? Of course, water is one of the basic elements in the Five Elements system.

REFLECTING BRILLIANCE

As with space, and we will see this repeated for each element, the wisdom properties of water can be seen in its physical properties. Water that gathers in pools, lakes, and ponds reflects light. In the stillness of the water we can see things clearly. The ancient Greek story of Narcissus describes the incredible experience of being able to see one's reflection, to have a glimpse of what was previously invisible: our own face.

Water also refreshes, bringing a parched landscape or being back to life. These days, people frequently talk of the need to "hydrate," and we are aware of the health benefits of staying watered. Through the wonder of capillary action, we can even watch this process of life-giving hydration as plants revive and take on a healthy, full posture after they have become droopy from the lack of water.

In the biblical wisdom literature, we are told that Wisdom is unfading and radiant (Wisdom 6:12), and what can be more radiant than a beautiful fresh morning when the dew is on the grass, the air smells fresh, and everything looks alive and healthy. These are the wisdom qualities of water: clarity, life-giving understanding, a sharpness and focus of mind, and a perspective that sees patterns: both the intricacy of the particular and also the overarching big picture. The color of water, not surprisingly, is blue, and its season is winter.

The wisdom of water is often described as being like the sight of an eagle that slowly circles the landscape at a huge height, seeing every detail, being able to pick out the smallest animal as it scurries from place to place. When we engage the wisdom of water, we are able to see and know things. This wisdom generates awareness and makes sense of vast amounts of data and information. People with water as their dominant energy are often scientists or engineers and are often described as highly intellectual.

If we consider a wide range of biblical stories, we see that many powerful spiritual encounters happen at the water wells in the desert. While this could simply be attributed to the fact that people would meet at wells, for they are a regular and important gathering place, from the perspective of a spiritual reading of Scripture, the clarity of water is being invoked to generate greater spiritual clarity. For water is the source of life, and few understand this better than a desert people. Thus, what better place to deliver spiritual wisdom than at a well? Perhaps the best example of this use of wells and water is the story of the woman at the well in the fourth chapter of the Gospel of John.

Here, Jesus meets a solitary woman, a woman who seems to have been excluded from society as she is at the well alone in the heat of the day, at the well which is identified as Jacob's. This places the encounter at the source of water, and thus life, for the whole people of God, the descendants of Jacob/Israel. Yet the woman is a Samaritan, and therefore she is identified as being the "other," as someone outside the religious fold of the Judeans, which is where Jesus comes from. As they begin to talk, the first part of their conversation is mired in confusion. She is confused that Jesus is even talking to her, for she is an outsider; and then there is confusion about what sort of water Jesus is talking about. Is he asking for a drink of material water? Or does he want her to ask for some other kind of water. By the end of the story, Jesus identifies himself with the Spirit of Life, with living water, and the woman is convinced that he is the Messiah because, as she later tells the villagers, of his ability to see her clearly and to tell her "everything she had ever done" (John 4:39).

As the story unfolds, we can see the wisdom of the energy of water at play in their interaction as well as in the teachings that are revealed. What begins as confusion—confusion that is a result of human division, the boundaries we create between ourselves, one another, and God—slowly begins to morph into clarity. Jesus sees all. He sees who she is; he sees what is needed for healing in the situation, and he sees what is to come: the worship of God in Spirit. The brilliant reflection of his mind is able to cut through the confusion and bring healing and a new view of human dignity and life. This is the power of the wisdom of water.

CUTTING THROUGH PROJECTION

In our individual and collective lives, this particular energy and wisdom quality has immense value. We have noted how our ego self spends most of its time and energy creating and maintaining projections—our delusional creations regarding the nature of the world around us. Once we generate these projections, we relate to them and become caught in an endless game of action and reaction where we are both the actors and the world we are acting within. This is the activity of the stick figure in the bubble. The projections are the movies we see on the inside of the bubble, and we engage the life we see without understanding that it is only a very partial view of reality as a whole. Plato's allegory of the cave[1] is another image of this life of projection: like those confined within the cave, we see only the shadows projected on the cave walls and act as if they are the real beings rather than shadows of reality.

This process of projection encourages and causes confusion. The woman at the well is confused by Jesus because his words and actions do not match the projections of her ego. Her life story tells her that men and women don't talk at wells, Judeans and Samaritans don't share water and conversation, and water is only material and not a living spiritual substance. When something from the world begins to poke through our projections, we are confused and struggle to maintain our understanding of reality. This is why talking across the "silos" of our lives is so hard. The silos are created by the projections of the individuals within the group, and the collective ego seeks to keep the walls of the silo intact. Interaction with members of another group risks having the projected structure collapse as new information and new pieces of reality enter our consciousness.

Water's wisdom seeks to dissolve these houses of sand. Allowing ourselves to relax into the space filled by life-giving, reflective water, we see and understand new things. Our projections can wash away and be replaced by a radiant view of reality, full of many possibilities and new patterns that we have not seen before. How many times can we look back on our lives and see paths that, going forward, we didn't know were there? Just like the molecules of water that can hold space for proteins hundreds of times bigger than they, so too, the wisdom of water holds us and our lives in a lattice of goodness and radiance. Compassionate relaxation allows us to see this structure and embrace it, and, as we do so, our lives become simpler, clearer, and more

---

1. There are many good websites that describe this allegory. See, for example, www.faculty.washington.edu/smcohen/320/cave.htm.

peaceful. Yet, when we relate to water energy from the neurotic perspective, we get quite the opposite results.

WATER NEUROSIS: THE VIOLENCE OF JUDGMENT

In the development of our ego selves, we noted that our mind uses a sorting system to handle the massive amounts of data it receives via our sense organs. Most of the data we ignore, and the rest we either put into either a "like" or "dislike" category. In the Buddhist tradition, these three categories are referred to as passion, aggression, and ignorance.[2] Because these approaches to our experience are central to the ego's life and action, each neurotic experience of an elemental energy is primarily driven by one of them. In describing the neurosis of space we saw that "ignorance" was the dominant cause of the neurotic aspects of that energetic relationship. For the water element, aggression is the primary ego approach that creates a neurotic experience.

Water is life giving, in appropriate amounts, but when unleashed with force, water is also one of the most destructive substances on the planet. As climate change gathers strength, one of its effects is the rise of more powerful storms. These massive atmospheric systems unleash the destructive power of water through tidal action, waves, and torrential downpours. Rainfalls of two to three feet are becoming more common and lead to more destructive flooding. Sea-level rise is now an inexorable global phenomenon, and the advance of the waters cannot be stopped. It is no wonder that throughout Scripture one of the

---

2. For an excellent description, see Dzogchen Ponlop Rinpoche, "The Wisdom of Emotions," *Tricycle*, October 5, 2018, www.tricycle. org. See also Dzogchen Ponlop Rinpoche, *Emotional Rescue: How to Work with Your Emotions to Transform Hurt and Confusion into Energy That Empowers You* (New York: TarcherPerigee/Penguin, 2016).

jobs assigned to God is the holding back of the waters, for this is something that humans cannot do forever.

As with the wisdom aspects of the elements, the neurotic aspects mirror the physical attributes of the respective element. The neurotic experience of water is that of violent, and destructive, judgment. We saw that the wisdom of water lies in a clarity of mind and a deep understanding of how things are arranged and work in the world. When we approach this energy and ability from the perspective of a non-ego state, when we allow God to be the beginning and end of wisdom, then we experience a life-giving power in the clarity. However, when we are trying to possess this knowledge and clarity, or when we feel we do not have the clarity we need, our ego reacts with tremendous aggression and violence toward ourselves and others.

The experience of "beating yourself up" is primarily the experience of water neurosis. We feel that we should have done something differently, we aren't smart enough, good enough, or beautiful enough, and we have somehow failed ourselves or others. This is the experience of the ego self separate from the wisdom of water, and we react with tremendous aggression toward ourselves, trying to grasp something that we fear we do not have. We feel this flagellation as a great flood of shame, anger, or self-loathing, and our innate compassion is drowned beneath this violent wave.

This habit of aggression toward oneself is generally conditioned by the experience of aggression—through some abusive or dysfunctional behavior—that one experienced as a child. When this happens, we receive a distorted, inaccurate view of ourselves, and we come to believe we are not worthy of life-giving nourishment. It is as if the water of life is removed from our being. This is the nature of the trauma response.

As we live this experience continuously, repeated thousands

of times throughout our childhood and beyond, we become like someone seeking water in the desert, a deer panting for water (Psalm 42:1), and we believe, through the delusional projection we have formed, that we will never receive what we need. Thus, every experience of this element, every experience of clarity, rather than being wisdom is felt as deprivation and fault. Without the balm of compassion, we, unconsciously and out of habit, turn an opportunity for nourishment into another opportunity for self-flagellation.

When water neurosis is turned outward, the aggression presents itself as anger, judgment, and tremendous self-righteousness. Our ego self is working to possess the wisdom and clarity of this energy, and those who are judged as inferior or "not getting it" are subject to its wrath. Within the religious world, fundamentalism is a perfect example of water neurosis at work on a collective scale.

A religion may have a particularly valuable insight or teaching, but, as the institutional ego grows, this received wisdom becomes a weapon against anyone who disagrees with or questions those who are part of the religious order. The intense focus on "right doctrine" within fundamentalist circles represents a perversion of the intellectual clarity that water brings. The aggression within such communities is obvious as they lash out at others and even turn against themselves with endless splits and divides, expelling from the community anyone who disagrees with their position. This is the source of religious and spiritual abuse, the anger and judgment of this neurosis codified into doctrines such as eternal damnation, which are then directed at the members as a way to terrify them into submission.

Two of the realms associated with water neurosis are the realms of hell and of jealous gods. Both of these realms are characterized by tremendous anger and aggression. In the former, these characteristics are self-directed, as in the beating-yourself-up example, and in the latter, the aggression is outwardly directed. The ego has become a jealous god, rampaging over the landscape fighting with the other gods for domination of the world. Today, much of our public discourse displays qualities of this realm when insights and knowledge are "weaponized" for discrediting or destroying an opponent. This behavior turns the clarity of water into a raging torrent, causing destruction where it should bring life.

MOVING FROM AGGRESSION TO CLARITY

Good news from far away is like cold water to the thirsty.
—Proverbs 25:25

The Christian wisdom tradition is full of contrasts between the wisdom of the world and the wisdom of God. Paul talks about this directly in his first letter to the Corinthians, turning the wise/foolish dichotomy on its head by pointing out that the wisdom of God seems as foolishness to the wisdom of the world (1 Corinthians 1:18–21). The wisdom he's referencing here is most likely the philosophy and religious teachings of the times, the intellectual wisdom of the Greek world. This is a reference to the intellectual wisdom that arises from the water element. As we've noted, however, and as the wisdom tradition affirms, when this wisdom is used at the service of the ego, it can move from being life giving to death dealing.

We certainly see this process in our modern relationships to the environment, and it lies at the heart of the climate crisis that is before us. Human arrogance born of alienation from our elemental nature is revealed in our repeated attempts to "engineer" the natural world from a position of lofty superiority, the results of which can range from the somewhat comic to the decidedly disastrous.

Years ago, when we were on the island of St. John in the Caribbean, we learned that the indigenous ecosystem contained no mammals. Those mammals who now inhabit the island are all invasive species. One of the first to arrive were rats, which came on the European ships and soon overran the island because there were no predators keeping their population in check.

The colonial government had heard that mongooses ate rats, and, secure in their superior knowledge, they introduced mongooses on the island. What they didn't think of was that the rats were largely nocturnal and the mongoose are diurnal. So these creatures never interacted; both populations flourished and, to make matters worse, the mongoose fed on the eggs of birds and turtles, effectively wiping out several indigenous species. This ecological tragedy was repeated throughout the Caribbean and the Pacific on several islands conquered by the Europeans, who were informed by a Christianity of alienation and environmental subjugation.

In the modern era, this attitude of superior knowledge continues with the advent of genetic manipulation and modification. In the agricultural arena, farmers were assured that genetically altered crops would solve the problems of weeds because the resistant crops could be sprayed with pesticides that would kill the undesirable plants in the fields. This promise was made despite the well-known fact that in plants genes "jump" from species to species, usually with the help of viruses. Now, after several years of the use of such technology, terrifying super weeds, which have the resistant gene, are populating wide swaths of the American Midwest, requiring ever more toxic chemicals to kill. Oh, and that benign pesticide, we are now learning, is a potent carcinogen.

But perhaps the best examples of the water neurosis that results from an ego-driven approach to wisdom are our relationship with water itself and our response to climate change. Across the world, sources of fresh water are being depleted and polluted at a terrifying rate. In the United States, the recent scandal in Flint, Michigan, saw its population poisoned by lead when the fresh water for the city was switched from a source that was clean to one that was so acidic that it dissolved the old lead supply pipes. New methods of oil extraction such as fracking and tar-sands mining pollute entire underground aquifers and discharge millions of gallons of contaminated wastewater into rivers and lakes. These activities, especially in the face of climate change when we should be extracting less oil and gas and taking care to preserve fresh water, show us how out of touch we have become with the wisdom of clean, clear water. And those who deny the climate crisis and intentionally sow confusion and promote blindness are manifesting the neurosis of water energy as they generate intense aggression against solutions or climate-change action.

The practice of embracing water's wisdom is the practice of moving from aggression toward self and others—this superiority complex in relation to knowledge of the world—to the clarity of the wisdom given by God. When we spend time with the element of water, our minds tend to settle and clarify naturally. Wisdom and goodness arise spontaneously as God is always trying to invite us to insight. In the Wisdom of Solomon, we hear that "wisdom meets us in every thought" (Wisdom 6:17). What a beautiful image. Wisdom is there, radiant, clear, of immense value, and always ready to gift us with the knowledge needed to address whatever challenge is before us.

To practice recognizing this wisdom, spend time near or with water. Notice how it feels to drink clean water, imagining your cells hydrating. If you don't have access to a real body of water, you can spend time with pictures of water or doing creative expression[3] with blue colors or other artistic media. In your healing work, be aware of situations that confuse you. Seek clarity from others; and, if you have a tendency to ignore compliments, practice listening deeply and letting in the truth of the love that is directed toward you. These are practices that allow the wisdom of water to enter your being and refresh you.

When we invite compassion into our experience, we are able to meet our thoughts and feelings not with aggression but with loving kindness. This is the basis of the elemental practice. The wisdom of water is often very simple and obvious. We know we need clean water to drink. This isn't profound, except when the truth of it is clouded by greed, aggression, hatred, and a lack of caring. How can the governor of a state poison an entire city without being possessed by the delusion of the realm of the jealous gods?

We must let go of the ego's proclivity that makes us feel as though we know more than the natural world and engage with our elemental nature to embrace this humbling posture. The water in our bodies exists in the bodies of billions of creatures. The water that flows through us flows into the world and back to other people, animals, and plants. Why would we want to hurt those creatures or do things to the environment that hurt us? As we continue our elemental practice, we recognize the innate wisdom that permeates creation, and we participate in this wisdom, not as conquerors but as co-creative servants, an observation that leads us to our next element, the one whose wisdom quality manifests action—the element of air.

---

3. The term "creative expression" refers to any creative activity that helps you pay attention to your experience. This can include journaling, drawing, sculpting, photography, dance, music, etc. The list is endless, explore!

7

The Wisdom of Air:
Compassionate Action

For she [Wisdom] *is a breath of the power of God, and a
pure emanation of the glory of the Almighty.*
—Wisdom 7:25

Two words that many modern parents live in fear of hearing are,
"I'm bored." In a society of constant movement and activity, it
seems the worst thing that a child can experience is boredom,
that state when we feel we have nothing to do and no clear sense
of what we'd like to do next. This childhood dislike of boredom, as the teenage years arrive, morphs into a blanket judgment on one's hometown or community: "There's nothing going
on here"; and this lingering uncertainty about action seems to
follow us everywhere. A parent in our town of 8,100 laughed as
he told me about his twenty-two-year-old son who had moved
to Los Angeles and recently announced, during a phone call
home, that "there's nothing to do here in LA!"

Frequently, in my individual healing work I ask, "What do
you want to do?" regarding a given situation or general direction
in life, and it is noticeable how many times the first answer is, "I
don't know." A lack of awareness regarding action is one of the
great paradoxes of our experience. Although we are constantly

acting, moving, doing, when we are given space to reflect on what we want to do, or why we do what we do, we are often at a loss. It appears life is like being on a conveyor belt to nowhere: it begins, we are told what to do and how to function in the world, we work and strive to survive as best we can, and then, eventually, it ends. We spend tremendous energy acting in the world, but why? And to sustain us through this activity, we breathe, taking in air, which provides us with the oxygen and energy to keep us going. In the Buddhist Five Elements teaching, air is the element of action, and its wisdom aspect has much to teach us about how we function for good in a world faced with extraordinary crises.

THE SPIRIT MOVES

Like space, air is an element that we cannot see but is all around us. The sphere of rock that is planet Earth hurls through space wrapped in a thin blanket of gas that, like water, nourishes the life grounded on the planet. The blowing wind, caused by the constantly changing atmospheric pressure as the air interacts with landscape and temperature variations, allows us to experience this element very directly even as we take it for granted. Of course, if we are met with a situation where we are suddenly deprived of oxygen, we become very aware of its existence. This element was regarded as so important by the ancient peoples who wrote the Bible that they visualized the Spirit of God as wind, breathing life into all creatures and moving at will throughout time and space to accomplish God's work in the world.

In the landscape of the plains, the wide-open space that encompasses much of the Midwest of the United States, the wind blows much of the time. John 3:8, which describes the wind's endless beginning and end—"The wind blows where it wills, and you hear the sound of it, but you do not know whence it comes or whither it goes"—could have been written there. In this environment, the movement of air is a constant reminder of its existence, and, even though it is an essential element, people tire of the unceasing movement and love the moments when there is perfect stillness and the sound of the rush of wind dies. In the Buddhist Five Elements system, the teachings on air reflect both this life-giving quality and also the quality of movement and action. The color for the air element is green, and the season connected to air is spring, the season of new growth and life.

All spiritual teachings give the act of creativity a central place in their reflections on the universe. Creativity, growth, life, creatures that reproduce themselves, the constantly changing seasons are among the most notable actions and most remarkable aspects of the world around us. While humans recognized that we have the capacity to manipulate the environment with tools and technology, we have also always recognized that we do not have the ability to start the life process. This capacity to "breathe life" into inanimate objects has always been assigned to God or to some force of action that is beyond our control.

In the biblical wisdom tradition, Wisdom, as already noted, is one of the main drivers of God's creative action. She is described as a "master worker" who is "beside God" as the world is formed and made (see Proverbs 8:30). The ability to direct the Spirit, to move and breathe the breath of life, is indeed a profound spiritual wisdom; and the ability to create a universe that is good and has an order that can manifest divine will is understood as one of the most important attributes of God.

In the Buddhist tradition, action is talked about as an endless stream of cause and effect, the law of karma (the Buddhist term for the air element). Interestingly, Buddhism is not concerned with primary origins, where did karma begin. This is reflective of Buddhism as a nontheistic religion, but the teachings reflect the ongoing creation of cause and effect, the momentum of action that we move through every day.

Air's wisdom, therefore, reflects the good, playful, loving action that is directed toward health and wholeness within individuals but also within groups and communities. Such action can be swift and decisive, but it can also be slow and patient. When the Bible uses phrases such as "the fullness of time" (Galatians 4:4) to describe the waiting and watching that proceeds the coming of Jesus, it reflects this wisdom of active waiting and movement that happens when it is appropriate and helpful.

The movement of God working in the world is how Christianity describes the ongoing creative action of the Divine that is always directing the universe toward the kingdom of God. Such action toward fulfillment is reflected in the movement of ecological systems toward their mature state of equilibrium. When ecologists describe the development of ecosystems, they note that a landscape or a waterscape undergoes a succession of species until it reaches a state where the ecology is populated by climax species in a balanced system. Old growth forests are an example of such a landscape.

When a new piece of land appears out of the ocean, as the result of volcanic action for example, it becomes populated with life. As the island grows and ages, new creatures and a succession of plants, birds, and animals arrive, providing fertilizer, creating soil, giving shelter or food to the next set of inhabitants. Over time, possibly hundreds of years, this land becomes one where creatures can grow and thrive and find a place for themselves. This process reflects the wisdom of compassionate, intelligent action blowing through time, nourishing creativity. This is no different from the biblical story that begins with the creation of the human being, moves through to the creation of the second human being, the Christ, and then looks forward to the development of the fullness of God's kingdom. Of course, such action is not simply linear—one way of viewing time and action—but it also occurs in cycles and rhythms of growth and decay, life and death. These cycles are also part of the wisdom of air.

When we embrace this wisdom, our lives align with the movement of the Spirit. We work with the flow of God in our lives, and we drop the struggle of our own individual ego actions and projects. But when this action of self dominates our lives, we encounter the neurotic expression of the air element: fruitless, destructive action.

AIR NEUROSIS: DEATH-DEALING ACTIVITY

The neurotic experience of the air element lies at the heart of the climate crisis, as it is central to the global capitalist project of endless growth. If we want to see this neurosis in action, we need look no further than our economic obsession with more, bigger, better, with no regard for consequences. The industrial capitalist vision of limitless expansion, driven by endless extraction of material resources for the production of more stuff that is then disposed of and replaced, is the quintessential picture of action without wisdom.

This is also reflected in the busyness of our society, which has reached such extreme levels that it is creating the autoimmune illnesses described earlier. And this phrenetic activity is supposedly in the name of being more efficient, more fulfilled, and of living our "best life" and the many other advertising slogans that are designed to encourage us to buy more in the name of economic expansion.

These reflect, on a societal scale, what happens when the ego self appropriates the energy of air for its own purposes.

The neurotic experience of air is action that is oriented toward ego gratification. This is the action of control, domination, and oppression. It is the action that sees everyone as an object to be manipulated and used. "It's not personal; it's business" is a slogan that summarizes this neurotic stance. When a company can destroy a community by moving a factory, or a coworker can betray a friend for a promotion, we see the ego acting to preserve and expand itself regardless of others and without a sense of compassion and care.

Like the element of water, air neurosis runs on the energy of *aggression* and can generate tremendous levels of paranoia and violence. Thus, war is also an expression of air neurosis and mimics the destructive action of violent wind, which wreaks havoc across a landscape. This collective violence is the ultimate expression of action without love; the insistence on control and maintenance of territory is so great that the ego of the tribe tries to obliterate the other.

These expressions reflect the habits that arise when we are trying to grasp air energy. When we are experiencing a lack of this element and our ego feels removed from the wisdom of action, we manifest another important experience of air neurosis that psychologists have termed *codependence*. This experience of disempowerment, which correlates with the lack of space given to these same groups, is most often felt by women in patriarchal societies—which unfortunately, exemplifies most societies throughout history—and also by oppressed people within a society. Here, the ego habituates to the experience of not being able to act in a wise way. In response, the person internalizes the oppression, and this manifests in action that perpetuates the disempowerment and harm.

One clear example of this process is the codependence of addiction. The spouse or partner of the addict continues to help them in their addiction or tries to get the addict to quit through useless complaints or "nagging." These actions are fruitless and result in nothing other than more harm to the addict's partner. Rather than empowering themselves to set boundaries and do what would be healthy for their own lives, such as leaving an unhealthy relationship and starting anew, the codependent person is disconnected from the wisdom of action that could allow them to be healthy.

A similar pattern of unhealthy internalization is evident in discussions on racism and colonialism. Those who are oppressed internalize the colonizers' teachings of the inferiority of the colonized. In the United States, African slaves and Native Americans were taught that their religion and their personhood were inferior to European, white Christianity. These teachings, as well as the trauma of slavery and genocide, have created an internalized oppression that still challenges people from these backgrounds when they feel empowered to act in their own lives and the lives of their communities.

Thus, we see that the neurotic expressions of our relationship to air can turn life-giving oxygen into death-dealing Category 5 hurricanes. Our ability to act in the world is one of our most precious gifts. As noted, the gift of *dominion* over the earth is one of the defining attributes of being human. When we use this gift from an ego perspective, we create the alienated action that is destroying our planet through the intersecting crises we are currently facing. The practice of elemental wisdom helps us move from action that defiles to action that uplifts.

DISCERNING COMPASSIONATE ACTION

When we take a deep breath, we can feel the oxygen giving life to our bodies. Who doesn't love stepping outside on a crisp, clear day and breathing in fresh, clean air? "Oh, the air smells so good," is a comment one often hears in a beautiful rural area where the air is perfumed by the trees and grass. Those fortunate enough to live or to have been to such places know what it's like to experience air in its pristine state.

Recently a delegation of professors from a typical Chinese industrial city came to visit the MICAH retreat center in northwest Minnesota. As they walked our paths through the beautiful countryside, they repeatedly commented on the beautiful blue sky and the lovely green meadows. Later, we learned from a friend who often works in China that the vision of "blue sky" is an almost mythological image embraced by city dwellers who see only concrete and grey and polluted air. I can imagine how wonderful it was to be in a place with endless, clean, beautiful sky surrounded by the green color of the air element.

The movement from ego-driven action to action governed by wisdom mimics the movement from polluted to fresh air; and as we engage in connecting with the wisdom of air, we can experience this life-giving transformation in our lives. Being in nature, in the fresh air, allows us to connect with the rhythms of Spirit-filled action. We become naturally attentive to the movements of the ecosystem we are visiting, the movement of the plants and animals around us, and the change in air movement from morning to evening.

When my wife and I kayak on Lake Superior, we become keenly aware of the change in wind conditions as the day heats and cools. In the morning, there is little breeze, because the land hasn't yet warmed from the day's sunshine. By early afternoon, the wind has picked up, raising waves on the waters of the lake. Then, as the evening approaches and the rays of the sun have less warmth, the thermal gradient, which stirred the wind, disappears, and the air over the land cools, causing the wind to die. Because of the power of the lake, we—small creatures in our little boats—need to respect this rhythm and move with it; to challenge the lake with our ideas about when to paddle could literally result in our death. But when we act in concert with the air, we experience the incredible beauty and energy of this life-giving activity.

In addition to a direct experience of the element, the Christian tradition has two powerful contemplative practices that work directly with the wisdom of air: *Sabbath* and *discernment*. The first, Sabbath, highlights the reality that wise action arises both from work and from rest. God instituted a time of spiritual reflection and practice and placed it within the flow of the week so that we could pause from endless outward doing and take a day to gain perspective and listen.

In a society governed by air neurosis, however, the practice and reality of Sabbath have been destroyed. Work now runs seven days a week, and "doing nothing" has become a cultural symbol of laziness and worthlessness. The Sabbath day has become just another day to "get things done" or run to our next activity, and even those who go to church have the expectation that they will get out of services exactly on time so that they can rush to their next appointment. Returning to Sabbath practice is one way to enter the wisdom of compassionate action, for it allows us to pause and reflect on ourselves and our lives and loosen the grip that the ego has on our endless running.

In the practice of discernment, the contemplative Christian tradition has a long history addressing the issue of action and what actions move in concert with God's Spirit. When I work with people individually in spiritual direction, we frequently return to this question: Is this (any given activity) life giving? For, if God's Spirit gives life, as Christianity and the Hebrew tradition before it has maintained for two thousand years, then, as we seek what is life giving, we are listening for the movement of the Spirit in our existence. We are looking for where the wind blows.

In the same way that elemental practice draws our awareness to the activity of ego versus the activity of enlightenment, or wisdom, so too discernment makes us aware of activity that brings life versus activity that bring death.[1] The beginning of discernment, which also is an essential posture for elemental practice, is cultivation of spiritual indifference. Indifference is a challenging concept, one that is often misunderstood to mean "not caring," lacking compassion, or being disengaged from the world. Nothing could be further from the truth.

Simply put, spiritual indifference is taking the position that I am always willing to let go of my ego habits: I am willing to see a broader view, entertain the notion that I am wrong; I am detached from my desired outcome in a given situation. This is a difficult place to reach, and our spiritual practice is what helps cultivate this attitude, which is essential for discerning wise action. On the one hand, if God's desires for me run counter to my ego's desires—a very common occurrence—and I cannot consider the situation with spiritual indifference, then I will never see what God is calling me to do. On the other hand, the more I live with indifference, the more I am open to the movement of the Spirit wherever it may blow. The second step in discernment is to reflect on actions as they unfold and ask ourselves whether the fruits of these actions are of the Spirit? In the Buddhist tradition, actions are considered and judged depending on whether they increase compassion and goodness in the world. These are very similar standards. If actions manifest the Spirit's

---

1. A full description of the practice of discernment is beyond the scope of this work. For an excellent starting place, see Elizabeth Liebert, *The Way of Discernment: Spiritual Practices for Decision Making* (Louisville, KY: Westminster John Knox Press, 2008).

fruits, if they increase love, peace, patience, healing, and the manifestation of wisdom, then we continue with these actions. They are life giving. However, if they manifest the fruits of the spirit of ego: anger, violence, war, the actions of the fool, then we stop them. While this decision making sounds simple, it is only possible from the perspective of indifference, for many of our habits are death dealing, yet we are attached to them and, therefore, struggle to see the negative fruits and to let go of the harmful actions.

The challenge of discernment is understandable when we look at the crises we are facing. We know that polluting water, air, and earth is death dealing. We know that slavery, genocide, and violence are wrong and are also death dealing. Yet, these activities are driven by both the individual and collective ego actions of humanity, and so they continue. We are attached to the endless growth model of life in a capitalist society. Yet our spiritual life and practice can give us the courage to let go of these habits and embrace new actions that help us breathe new life into the systems we inhabit.

One of the most powerful actions we can take in the face of the climate crisis is to consider our air element using the practices outlined above. Listening for how the Spirit is blowing in our lives, and boldly taking action to change how we live, is empowering and fulfilling. Although we are constrained by the many systems of the world, ultimately you are the only person that you can control, and reflecting the wisdom of air brings life to one's personal world and also the wider world.

Like the wisdoms we have already explored, the next element will further aid us in this bold work, for the wisdom of earth grounds us on our planet and fills us with the essentials for what lies ahead.

8

The Wisdom of Earth: Grounded in Abundance

Take my instruction instead of silver, and knowledge rather than choice gold; for wisdom is better than jewels, and all that you may desire cannot compare with her.
—Proverbs 8:10–11

It was impossible to be an organic vegetable farmer and not be impressed, almost daily, by earth's abundance. The amount of produce I harvested out of my very small farm often threatened to overwhelm my ability to handle and process it. This bounty also confronted the absurdity of putting food production within a capitalist economic system. If I always had more and more produce, wouldn't my price eventually drop to zero? Going to the market to sell a few pounds of cauliflower for a price that would at least cover my costs, and then coming home to a dozen more heads that weren't "perfect" but were delicious and that I gave away or froze, always seemed strange. The earth produces as much as we need.

The earth is also the incredible place we get to inhabit. Gravity, that still unexplained property of matter that allows for the interconnection and interaction of the "heavenly bodies," is another aspect of our universe we take for granted, yet it provides life with a home. Our family loves sharing the story of my eldest son, who at the age of four was first told about gravity by my dad. They were outside at our farm playing, and I was inside when suddenly Sam ran in and exclaimed, "There's gravity out there!" We have heard about the challenges of working and living in space where there is no gravity, how our bodies begin to deteriorate and how so many basic life functions are difficult if not impossible. Without gravity, and the electromagnetic fields that surround the earth, plants won't grow, cells won't differentiate, and movement is impossible. Being grounded is a tremendous gift that allows the abundance of life.

Earth is such an important element that the biblical creation story notes that we are made of dust, and every year on Ash Wednesday, Christians remind one another of our dusty origins and destination. The Five Elements theory also recognized the essential nature of earth and the wisdom that can be found around us and beneath our feet.

UNENDING ABUNDANCE

Throughout the biblical wisdom tradition, Wisdom personifies abundance. She is more valuable than silver and gold, more precious than jewels. No earthly thing compares with her and her value; having her is similar to having unending riches. In the Five Elements theory, abundance—physical, psychological, and spiritual—is also a quality of wisdom, and earth is the element through which this attribute is revealed. The color of the earth element is bright yellow, and the season most reflecting earth qualities is the fall—the season of harvest.

In the Genesis 1 account of creation, the first three elements, space, water, and air, appear and set the stage for the next acts of creation. As the earth comes forth from the waters, creation of land-based life is made possible. Then earth is the foundational element by which God creates human beings in God's image. Earth is also the container that holds the waters below and therefore provides nurture for even the sea creatures. Of course, creatures need to eat, and from where will this food come, if not the earth? In most faith communities I've visited or belonged to, it often goes unnoticed that, originally, in Eden, all creatures were vegetarians, eating the plants that sprang forth from the earth. Such is the material abundance of earth that, in God's creative play, there is provision for every being who comes into existence.

The wisdom of earth is the wisdom of enough: enough time, enough food, enough nurture. It is also the teaching that speaks to us of the goodness of our inherent being: the image of God within is good and is good enough. We are fully loved for who we are, and we do not need to "do" more to have abundant value. The wisdom of enough recognizes that all we need is available to us and to every human on the planet. Many who work in the area of food security have discussed and described this truth; there is plenty of food for everyone. The problem isn't quantity; rather, it is our lack of ability to share that causes the phenomenon of starvation and deprivation.[1]

People who manifest the earth element and energy as their primary wisdom love abundance of food, decor, and color, and there is a rich sensuousness and nurturing quality that emanates from them. These are the people whose house is richly decorated or who love to throw dinner parties and cook for everyone. This element manifests in the biblical "feeding" stories and in the importance of church suppers and potlucks. It is notable that

---

1. World Economic Forum, "The World Produces Enough Food to Feed Everyone. So Why Do People Go Hungry?," July 11, 2016, www.weforum.org.

most religions have a significant feeding ritual at the heart of their worship life. This is an intentional manifestation of the earth's elemental wisdom of abundant life; God feeds us both figuratively and literally.

Italy is a wonderful example of a culture whose primary energy is that of the earth: the endless supply of incredible food, art, and wine; cathedrals where every square inch of space is decorated, painted, or sculpted; and the art and music that is a ubiquitous presence in almost every public space; all manifests the bounty of earth. From the perspective of the earth element, the Reformation, with its desire to rid churches of statues, frescos, and paintings, missed the point. This elaborate ornamentation was not about worshiping idols but rather about appreciating the abundance of the Divine, a fullness you can feel in these remarkable spaces.

Another religious practice that manifests the energy of earth is the veneration of relics. Pieces of the bodies of saints—usually hair or bits of bone, or their clothing—are kept and displayed in beautiful reliquaries where the faithful can pray in their presence. For many, especially in our modern world, this practice appears bizarre or disgusting, yet it points to a significant understanding about the interaction between Spirit and our earthly bodies.

The Incarnation, the theological assertion that in Jesus God becomes enfleshed, entering into our material lives for the purpose of new life, is one of the most important teachings of Christianity. And if saints are people whose lives are defined by a powerful unitive relationship with God, then even their earthly, bodily matter is filled with the Spirit. Veneration of relics, in its best sense, is a deep prayerful reflection on the wisdom of earth, that the elemental stuff of which we are made is not inanimate but rather alive with the energy of the Divine.

The wisdom of earth also manifests in our relationship with material wealth, something that biblical wisdom frequently addresses. The abundance of God is something that flows through and around us, feeding and nurturing us but then moving on to other beings. This is the ecology of composting; the earth is an endless living recycling machine where the next generation of beings are fed by the previous generation. Plants and animals take turns transforming the gases of air into the solids of earth for the benefit of all beings. These ecological teachings are reflected in the spiritual teachings on wealth and money, which admonish us to not hold onto wealth but rather to give it away. This is why the rule of life guiding spiritual communities across religions has some form of vow of poverty or collective sharing of resources. People who live in these communities, as well as those who regularly tithe as part of their spiritual lives, experience what, from the perspective of worldly society, seems an absurd paradox: the more you give away, the more you have. Yet, this is a manifestation of earth's wisdom. As we allow ourselves to enter fully into the movement of living energy as it flows through our material reality, we experience the divine abundance. Yet, when our ego self becomes separated from this energy, we move into the realm of endless desire and we meet the hungry ghosts.

Earth Neurosis: Nothing Is Ever Enough

If the wisdom of earth is abundance, then the neurotic experience of this element is poverty, the experience of never having enough. In saying this, let's be very clear that we are not talking about the literal poverty that arises in societies from inequality and the mechanisms of oppression that humans routinely employ on one another. This is not some form of prosperity gospel or New Age version of "just think positively and you will manifest anything you want." These teachings are perversions of wisdom teachings that blame people for their negative experiences, and even shame them into thinking, for example, that they got cancer because they didn't pray properly, or that "God wants" them to have a house they cannot afford so they should take out a risky mortgage that drives them into bankruptcy. In fact, such teachings are really a manifestation of earth neurosis, and the wisdom and abundance of earth empower us to seek justice by working to change the systems that hold people in a poverty that is counter to God's desire for humanity. Rather, we are talking about a much deeper, far more basic stance that we take in relationship with ourselves and the world.

As with the other elements, our ego self relates to the basic elemental energy from a perspective either of lacking that energy or of trying to grasp or control that energy for itself. When this process occurs in relation to the energy of abundance, we enter into a realm that Buddhist teachings describe as the realm of the hungry ghosts. These are beings with long thin necks and distended stomachs. There is an iron band around their neck that keeps them from eating much, and so they wander the earth, constantly hungry, trying to nourish themselves even as they are continually starving.

Every product commercial is intentionally trying to create this state of endless starvation. As we watch the beautiful happy people cavort on the beach or see the new car zoom along through the woods, our sense of inadequacy and desire is stimulated. If only we had that car or that vacation, we would finally be happy. Shopping channels parade an endless stream of beautiful things before our eyes, and now millions of people spend time before a screen buying things they do not need, or even want, hoping to feel satisfied. Of course, what we end up with is more junk, more credit card debt, and the desire to do it again.

It is the neurosis of the earth energy that drives our society toward endless accumulation, which, of course, involves the literal endless extraction from the earth. If the energy of air, action, is the mechanism that allows for the endless activity of extraction, it is the energy of earth, and the desire that arises when we are disconnected from this energy, that drives the activity. For earth neurosis is connected to the "like" category of our ego's sorting system. This is the quality of *passion*. We want things; our ego desires to possess, hoard, keep, grasp. In the biblical teachings, this is the sin of coveting: I want my neighbor's stuff. It is also the motto of the entire industrial world: if a little is good, more is better. It's not enough to be able to produce a few things a day through the work of a skilled artisan; no, we must design a machine and build a factory that can produce thousands of these things so that we can sell even more of them.

When the ego self feels that it is in possession of the earth element, it manifests the neurosis of endless domination and possession. This is the energy of imperial accumulation. In our modern day, the discussions of the "one percent," those people who own phenomenal amounts of wealth, are discussions related to this aspect of earth neurosis. From the perspective of ordinary human life, it is inconceivable that one would want, or think one needs, billions of dollars. These are sums that are completely unimaginable and serve only to prop up enormous egos even as they decimate the earth through the exploitation of millions of people whose basic needs aren't met even as they live in the shadow of enormous wealth.

The danger of this neurotic style is a frequent focus of biblical prophets and teachers. Jesus tells the story of the man who builds so many barns to store his wealth yet dies one night never getting the chance to appreciate it (see Luke 12:15–21). Isaiah rails against those who remove the poor from the land simply to create larger farms and a desolate landscape (Isaiah 5:8), a highly relevant teaching for today, as we witness the growth of industrial agriculture across the world, a practice that uses the earth with an eye toward maximum industrial efficiency even as it decimates human communities and pollutes the very earth on which it depends.

Jesus, who is endlessly manifesting the abundance of God as he feeds thousands, heals dozens, and finally offers even his own self for the renewal of the world, summarizes the choice between the wisdom and neurosis of the earth element when he states that one can either worship God or money, but not both (Matthew 6:24).

But earth neurosis isn't only about material items and our relationship with matter, it also has significant spiritual and psychological components.

If the experience of abundance allows us to recognize our inherent worth—that who we are is enough—then, when our ego self experiences the realm of the hungry ghosts, we enter into that delusion that we are not enough. We aren't good enough, lovable enough, pretty enough, spiritual enough. These feelings of lack are what drive billion dollar self-help industries, make-up industries, and weight-loss industries.

But perhaps the most tragic manifestation of earth neurosis is the religious teachings that endlessly focus on human failure and inadequacy. These are the churches whose teachings focus on sin more than salvation, that teach us that women are somehow inferior and cannot preach or lead, and claim that some people, because of their skin color, religion, or sexual orientations, are hated by God and will go to hell. It often appears that, in these communities, evil and Satan have far more power than God; and people are always encouraged to feel afraid, alone, and distant from divine favor. This, of course, is exactly the opposite of what Jesus and Wisdom teach. Repeatedly, Jesus comes to the person who has been given nothing by society and shows God's love and favor to that person. And the wisdom teachings of the book of Proverbs are presented so that it's clear they are available to all without preference. Recognizing abundance is the experience of moving from the neurotic spiritual poverty of earth to its wisdom aspect.

Coming to the Banquet

I have witnessed many moments when a person, for the first time, has the experience that they are truly loved by God and are deeply connected to the entire universe. These are times of great joy, awakening, and transformation, and they are examples of the shift that can occur in our consciousness when we move from the neurotic experience of earth into its wisdom manifestation.

Working with the earth element is at the heart of creating an embodied spirituality, for our bodies are of the stuff of the earth. In response to a traumatic event, and as a means of protection, our minds become disconnected from our bodies to avoid pain, but this creates an enduring rift within ourselves, which is the ongoing legacy of trauma. When we are "triggered," the term that refers to an experience that recalls the memory of the traumatic event, we again flee from our bodies and are sent into a state of fear, anxiety, and pain. Activities that allow us to enter into our bodies in a loving and healing way are at the heart of effective trauma treatment.

Engaging the earth element helps us to come into our embodied reality and experience God's ever-present abundance. Meditation practices are deeply embodied, drawing us into our bodies and helping us experience ourselves as earthly beings, grounded on the planet, rooted in the soil, tied to the rest of the earth through that magical force of gravity. This is why spi.. tual teachings encourage us to practice meditation frequently, because our contemplative engagement undoes the legacy of trauma in our bodies and allows us to move toward wisdom and be nourished.

In chapter 3, we briefly discussed how, as Christians, one of our biggest challenges is the legacy of negative teachings about our bodies and embodiment. This legacy makes it hard to move toward earth wisdom. Sadly, these teachings, like the impoverished fearful teachings mentioned above, are at variance with incarnational faith. While there are many theories about why religion is often negative, and even abusive, toward our body, these tendencies, which, despite some assertions to the contrary, can be traced back through human history, arise from our ego's basic fear of death. This is the same fear of extinction that helps to create our alienated faith.

Once we recognize that we are alive, we become terrified by our impending nonexistence, the grief we experience when we lose loved ones, and the basic pain that comes naturally as a result of having a body that grows old and experiences illness. Since the natural defense mechanism of the ego is projection, these deep emotional experiences are projected onto our own body, which we deem the source of our distress. This process eventually becomes encoded into religious doctrine and practice, and yet, rather than being true and real, it is merely another manifestation of the traumatic experience of being human.

Allowing ourselves to relate deeply to the element of earth brings with it an experience of calm and joy at our embodiment. We realize that we are the stuff of the universe, the star dust of popular song and science fiction; and this realization shifts the experience of our embodiment from alienation and pain to one of integrated wholeness.

Any practice that brings us out of our thoughts and into reality can help with the movement from earth neurosis to wisdom. One suggestion is to spend time lying on the ground and feeling the solidity of the earth beneath or leaning against a tree. One person I worked with, whose primary energy is the earth energy and who spent much of their time feeling inadequate, told me that they had recently moved to a new house. One of the attractions of this house, not surprisingly to me, was the beautiful piece of woods beyond the backyard. As part of our work together, I told them to go into the woods, find a tree they liked, and spend time sitting up against the tree. After several weeks of this practice, the person reported that they were feeling much better and calmer. Their angry outbursts had greatly decreased, and their self-confidence and happiness had increased; they were experiencing their earth energy as abundance and not as deficiency.

Other practices that can help us experience earth wisdom include any type of physical activity that draws our awareness to our bodies: contemplative body practices, practicing generosity toward ourselves and others, donating things, gardening, and contemplative eating practices such as Slow Eating. These activities bring us into a direct and healing relationship with the earth, the opposite of our current global relationship to the planet.

The climate crisis we are experiencing is a direct result of our collective experience of a neurotic relationship to the earth. There is currently more "stuff" on the planet than we could ever use or need. We could cease all industrial production tomorrow and probably exist with the stuff we currently have for decades. Imagine the instant and radical decrease in carbon dioxide emissions! We can see the truth of this gross excess surrounding us: mini-storage units appearing everywhere like weeds, the endless hours we spend cleaning closets, the flooding of Africa and South America with excess clothing from well-meaning American Christians that results in the bankruptcy of local merchants, and, my personal favorite, the garage sale culture, which moves objects around communities with stunning efficiency. There's so much stuff that, in small towns across the United States, you can sell your old items at your garage sale and then buy them back at a sale across town several years later.

The problem, of course, is that any action to stop our endless search for "more" would destroy our economy as it is currently constituted. It requires a radical shift in how we live our lives, spend our time, and distribute the resources of the earth. Such a shift is exactly what every spiritual tradition calls for and what deeply mature spiritual communities manifest. The biblical wisdom tradition calls for a life that is grounded in relationship with wisdom and a way of life that allows God's presence and abundance to flow through us and out into others. Instead of spending our time wandering the world as hungry ghosts, we are called to live simply, focusing on the basic work of community and spending much of our time in loving service to ourselves, others, and God. Entering deeply into this state of loving relationship is the subject of our next element: fire.

9

The Wisdom of Fire: Love for All

God is love.
> —1 John 4:7

Fire and heat are two of the defining signs of the climate crisis. In the Amazon of South America, in the vast expanses of Siberia, across North America, Australia, and Europe, forests are burning at a pace never before seen. Global temperature rise is, of course, *the* indicator of climate change, and every year we are seeing new temperature records set across the globe. As I write, the power companies in California are shutting off power to customers because, in 2017 and 2018, fires associated with downed power lines burned hundreds of thousands of acres and, for the first time in California's history, burned deep into urban areas, in one case destroying, almost completely, the town of Paradise. There is no greater symbol for the crisis we are facing than the "most powerful country in the world" sending its population back to the time before electricity because we might burn to the ground.

Yet fire is also wonderful. As a child, I learned how the "taming of fire" was one of the great accomplishments of early humans. Sitting around a fire is a timeless activity that feels wonderful, creates community, and brings a sense of safety and belonging.

Fire has also been invaluable to the creation of human civiliza-
tion and has served us in a myriad of ways. Cooking, metal
working, chemistry, engines, electricity, and light, the list is
endless, all depend on the transformative power of fire.

On a more microscopic level, fire is simply the outward
manifestation of a chemical, or nuclear, reaction. It is the movement of energy. Fire becomes visible when a reaction produces
more energy than it consumes. This extra energy needs to go
somewhere and appears in the material world as heat. If there's
enough heat, and if there is oxygen available and some other element or compound nearby that can react with the oxygen, then
fire appears. Living systems "harness fire" because they harness
energy. Every living organism needs energy to survive, and cells
have developed hugely complex systems of enzymes and microscopic structures designed to facilitate the production and use of
energy for the purpose of self-maintenance.

The energy released in fire also gives light. In the account of
creation in Genesis 1, the appearance of light is the result of the
first words spoken by God. Then throughout the biblical stories,
light is used repeatedly to indicate the presence of the Divine,
even to the extent that Jesus identifies himself as light (see John
8:12). We know how important light is in a practical sense, and
the ability to "see one's way" is a central image in the spiritual
life across traditions. Fire, like the other elements, is basic to life
on earth and the reason it appears as one of the five elements in
Five Element theory.

Loving Relationship

The psychological and spiritual dimension that underlies these
life-giving properties of fire is love, and loving relationship. Fire
is a physical manifestation of the energetic bonds that hold life
together, make life possible, provide the light that guides us, and

allow plants to form solids out of gases. What better word than love helps us to understand and describe the bonds that make our existence possible?

In the Five Element system, the wisdom of fire is the wisdom of loving relationship. Fire wisdom exhibits the properties of sensuality, connection, attraction, and the desire to support oneself and others. Acts of caring, altruism, sexuality, intimacy, and the intense attachments we feel toward those we love are all manifestations of the fire element. It is perhaps not surprising that the color associated with this element is red, and the season of fire is summer, with its light and warmth.

Love is central to the biblical narrative and the theology of the Christian faith. Not only is God described as love, but God's actions are described as loving, fueled by God's care and desire for humans to experience a good life. Jesus is described as loving his disciples, his friends, and the world. Although, unfortunately, the practice of religion is often devoid of love, there is no question that the intent of religion is to manifest love in the world.

In the Christian contemplative tradition, the centrality of love and its connection to fire are even clearer. Saints are often said to radiate light, and they describe their unitive experiences of God in terms of light and fire. The spiritual path itself is called the illuminative path, and John of the Cross titles his poem describing union with God "The Living Flame of Love."[1]

In the Buddhist tradition, loving kindness is the goal and result of one's spiritual life and practice. Meditation spontaneously opens the heart and allows us to become more loving and compassionate, qualities of an enlightened mind. This loving, compassionate quality is so powerful that a Bodhisattva, an

---

1. John of the Cross, *The Complete Works of Saint John of the Cross*, trans. E. Allison Peers (Westminster, MD: Newman Press, 1964).

enlightened teacher, is defined as someone who could simply disappear into the enlightened realm but instead chooses to remain on earth because they have so much compassion for the suffering of the rest of humanity. Love ties them to all beings.

Like the bonds that hold life together, love—the wisdom of fire—also appears to hold and sustain our existence. The power of love is what drives sexual reproduction, and thus literally maintains the species; and if we look at art, literature, and music, we see an ongoing stream of energy related to the need and desire for loving relationship. Indeed, quotes on love and the power of love to motivate people's action and choices fill hundreds of books. This is a testament to the power and essential nature of this element.

Those who have fire energy as their dominant element place great value on *caring*, *relationship*, and *feelings*. They radiate warmth and sensuality, and gravitate toward community. The extroverted expression of this energy manifests in those with many friends; they are "people" persons, who are continually interacting with others and are involved with many groups who desire to be of help. They care deeply about all things and know the world through their feelings. This energy is associated with emotional intelligence, and those who are empathic often have fire as their dominant energy.

When we are connected to the wisdom of fire, we feel loved and supported. We know that "all manner of things will be well."[2] As we read the book of Proverbs and the Wisdom of Solomon and hear the description of Wisdom, we can feel her warmth, her caring, her richness, and her desire to give us life and goodness. "Wisdom is radiant and unfading, and she is

---

2. Julian of Norwich, *Revelation of Divine Love (Short Text and Long Text)*, trans. Elizabeth Spearing (London: Penguin Books, 1999), 22.

easily discerned by those who love her, and is found by those who seek her" (Wisdom 6:12). Connected to this radiance, we can feel the energy flow within and without us, through the people to whom we connect, and the spiritual energy that moves in and around our heart and mind. We also enter into the realm of *enlightened selflessness*, that state of caring and service that emanates from us as we are nourished by love. This issue of self and service is discussed further below, especially how it can morph into a neurotic expression of the fire element when we are taught that our desires are merely selfish.

The wisdom of fire also recognizes another helpful property of fire—*purification*. The science and practice of metallurgy are made possible because the various compounds that comprise metal ores melt at different temperatures and react with oxygen differently. When an ore is exposed to extreme heat, the non-metallic compounds, the dross, burns away, and the pure metal can be separated and collected; a dull rock of ore can be transformed into a beautiful ingot of gold. This image of the refiner's fire is found in biblical narratives (Malachi 3:2, for example), and is used to convey the idea that God acts on us to remove the dross of our ego selves and reveal the golden image of God that lies buried beneath our habitual patterns.

This image of purification also arises as John the Baptist proclaims that Jesus will baptize with the Holy Spirit and fire (see Matthew 3:11). Here, again, we have the image of fire as an element of profound change; the human being can enter into new life, an image that is found in many spiritual traditions. In the story of the phoenix, the mythical Greek bird, the old bird is consumed by fire, and the new bird arises from the ashes. In the Buddhist Five Wisdom teaching, fire, as the element of love and compassion, can purify any claustrophobic ego space and allow us to step out into a new space of loving kindness. However, when the ego tries to harness fire for its own purposes, we are born into the most painful realm of all, the *human realm*.

FIRE NEUROSIS: THE SUFFERING OF THE HUMAN REALM

In our modern era of devastating forest fires, we are appreciating better the value of fire in the evolution of an ecological system. Our practice of suppressing fires has led to forests that are overflowing with dead trees, brush choking the forest floor, and thick layers of dead grasses and branches covering every inch of ground. In a nonhuman controlled ecosystem, these would be burned away on a regular basis by small fires that actually help the living trees grow by giving them more space in the forest. But human-controlled fire suppression leads to forests with too much fuel, and, when fires do erupt, they burn so hot that the living trees are killed. Purification is transformed into devastation as human beings, driven by our idea that we have more wisdom than the nonhuman natural world, try to impose our will upon the earth.

The neurosis of the fire element is the neurosis of unhealthy relationship: with ourselves, one another, and God. Rather than allowing space for loving relationship to emerge naturally, our ego, trying either to grasp love or feeling far from love, seeks to control this energy, which results in the suffering of human attachment. The Rock-and-Roll industry is based largely on this neurotic relationship with the fire element, and you can hear the cry of unsatisfied, heartbroken people grasping for love only to end up experiencing sorrow.

The human realm, which is the place of the neurotic fire experience, is what we experience in our daily lives. This is the realm of both caring and betrayal, of love and hatred, of great friendship followed by alienation and stony silence. The mod-

ern practice of "ghosting," in which a friend or business associate suddenly vanishes and won't respond to your calls, texts, or
emails, has become rampant within our culture and is a perfect
image of the ego-driven relationship with fire wisdom.

The neurosis of fire is manifest in dysfunctional relationships,
families, organizations, and societies; and trauma is the result of
actions driven by neurotic fire behavior. When our ego is in the
grip of a claustrophobic fire experience, the warmth and caring
of this element changes into a raging inferno that lashes out
with destructive behavior, often directed at those we love.

When the ego feels that it cannot grasp the fire element or
when it is about to lose the love and care it thinks it needs,
it reacts defensively in anger or collapses into self-deprecating
shame and hatred.

These patterns of behavior are particularly found in men
within patriarchal systems, a pattern recently termed "toxic
masculinity."[3] Patriarchy teaches men to disregard their hearts,
their emotions. They are trained to become "hard" in order to
commit the violent and oppressive acts required within the
patriarchal system. The role of managing emotions is given to
women, and when men feel their emotions aren't being appro-
priately managed, they become violent because they have to
face the pain of their own crushed humanity and will do anything to avoid this encounter. This highly dysfunctional pattern of behavior is what accounts for the incredibly high rates
of domestic violence in all societies, as well as the organized
social oppression of women. It is a highly toxic manifestation
of fire neurosis.

---

3. For an excellent summary, see Colleen Clemens, "What We
Mean When We Say, 'Toxic Masculinity,'" December 11, 2017, www.
tolerance.org.

The biblical wisdom tradition is full of descriptions of deceptive and duplicitous relationships in which people manipulate each other for gain, and a relationship that appears loving is simply a trap for abuse. These are also descriptions of the neurosis of fire—descriptions of a human society far from God—where people try to possess the love that is meant for all.

Unfortunately, Christianity has been one of the sources of a neurotic fire experience in its teachings on the human being, selfishness, and hell. Many people suffer from a deeply negative view of themselves. They spend much of their time caught in habitual patterns that denigrate who they are and ignore what they would really love to do in the world. From my clinical experience, the majority of such people are women. When I suggest that they pay attention to their desires, needs, and priorities, one of the first thoughts that arises is that such actions are selfish. Tracing the origin of this idea indicates that it often stems from teachings they received at church or through their family and the patriarchal society in which we live. Often raised in fundamentalist churches, they were repeatedly told that human beings are bad and sinful and that their own desires are corrupt and evil. As such, they are not worthy of love but rather punishment.

These instructions are a perversion of the wisdom of fire and for centuries have been used against people to control them through the fear of hell, a place where the warmth of fire is turned into a permanent torture chamber. The idea that a God who is love could construct such a place and then send the majority of humanity there can be maintained only by a feat of Orwellian doublespeak: love really means hate.[4]

---

4. For deeper reflections on Scripture and hell, see Randy Klassen, *What Does the Bible Really Say about Hell? Wrestling with the Traditional*

The result of this formational process is that generations of people have been traumatized into believing that they are not worthy of love, that they cannot pursue what they love, and that every thought and feeling of loving desire needs to be suppressed and ignored. This constellation of ego habit is a recipe for illness, psychological suffering, dysfunctional relationships, and all the problems that arise out of our inability to connect with the wisdom of fire in a direct, spacious, and open manner.

Buddhist teachings describe the human realm as the most painful. This is because the suffering engendered by a neurotic relationship with love, which is also suffering that arises from the ego habit of passion, is so difficult. The human realm, however, is also seen as the most important realm because it is only when we are human that we can hope to wake up to enlightenment; animals or gods cannot become wise. It is therefore fitting to end the exploration of the elements with a description of the movement from the neurosis of fire to the experience of its wisdom.

From Suffering to Love

> Therefore thou didst provide a flaming pillar of fire
> as a guide for thy people's unknown journey,
> and a harmless sun for their glorious wandering.
> —Wisdom 18:3

The spiritual life is often described as a journey. Engaging in our spiritual practice, we wander through the mystery of our existence searching for a deeper relationship with the Divine, a

---

View, in *Living Issues Discussion*, vol. 2 (Kitchener, ON: Pandora Press, 2001). For a theological reflection, see Daniel Wolpert, *The Collapse of the Three Story Universe: Christianity in an Age of Science* (Crookston, MN: MICAH, 2013), 85–93.

relationship that will bring healing, love, and an experience of life-giving connection. In earlier chapters, we noted the alienation of our current human existence, the pervasive loneliness that haunts so many in modern society, and the disconnection from self, other, and the environment that defines modern living. These are the experiences of the human realm, defined as a neurotic relationship with fire, but a life of spiritual practice slowly allows us to move from this experience of suffering to one of love. This is the life of the Spirit.

The Pentecost story (see Acts 2) presents the image of the tongues of fire as a visual affirmation that the Holy Spirit is inhabiting the disciples, giving them new powers of speech and transforming them. When the disciples receive this gift, they morph from clueless bumblers into powerful spiritual leaders, and this too is an image of the shift that happens as we go from an ego-driven relationship with fire to one of spaciousness and relaxation. This change recalls the promises of Ezekiel, where we hear that God will put a new heart into God's people (Ezekiel 36:26), a heart that is wise of its own accord. Not surprisingly, the heart is where love and the energy of fire resides in the Five Elements system.

When we spend more time with the element of fire, we can feel its warmth and heat nourish us and direct us toward Spirit-filled activity. We can do this by engaging directly with the element—sitting next to a fire or a candle, being out in the sunshine, or being near a sunlamp in the winter—or by engaging in other contemplative practices that connect us to our hearts such as loving-kindness meditation. In this practice, we spend time focusing loving, compassionate energy first to ourselves, then to others we know, and then to the entire world.

We also connect with the wisdom of fire through loving service. As noted earlier, this isn't service that comes at a neurotic

cost to self. We can often tell when we are engaged in that type
of service if we notice ourselves using the word "should" in relation to our undertaking. When we allow these "shoulds" to control our behavior, we engage in service that is compulsive and
ego driven because we don't wish to be selfish and nurture our
own desires. Such service only does damage to both ourselves
and others.

Sadly, much charity work falls into this category of service.
Well-meaning people who are "fortunate" wish to "give" to those
who are "less fortunate." Often, these activities come with large
imbalances in power and have little regard for the long-term consequences of the charitable actions. I've already mentioned the
example of dumping clothes from the United States around the
world, and how this does far more harm than good because it
puts local tailors out of business. Many "mission projects" fall
into this category. For example, I once attended a talk where a
person who ran a clinic in Guatemala showed pictures of rooms
full of broken and useless medical equipment that groups had
brought with them and dumped in the clinic, thinking they were
helping by bringing modern equipment to the poor. This is service that comes out of the ego's desire to feel good about helping.

The wisdom of love, the wisdom of fire, desires service that
is mutual and egalitarian. We serve not because we are better
and special but rather because genuine service is a gateway to
authentic relationship. If we cannot learn from those we serve,
we cannot form truly loving spiritual communities. This is true
of both the human and the nonhuman worlds.

About a decade ago, I was rehabilitating a six-acre hill, changing it over from monocropped farmland to prairie. After seeding
it, we got some rain, and between the runoff and an underground
spring, an area of erosion created a fissure in the hillside. Some
of my neighbors were distressed about this gash in the hill and

advised me to use a large piece of equipment to fill the hole. This desire represented a particular habitual pattern in relation to the land: humans know what is right and good and should manipulate the environment as they see fit. It is a relationship of power, not mutual listening. However, I felt that the hillside would know how to heal itself and work with this area caused by the running water. Over the years, this spot has evolved into one of my favorite spots on the hillside. Large trees grow near the natural spring, which has created a round, sheltered, quiet area where animals come to drink, and you can sit and quietly meditate. It's beautiful. The land knew what it needed and what it was doing, and by listening to its wisdom, a loving and beautiful place was created. This story is not only about the fire element, the element of loving relationship, it also contains aspects of earth and water. Noticing, understanding, and working with the relationships between elements is an essential aspect of the Five Wisdom teaching, which we return to in a later chapter.

In addition to developing a loving relationship with the environment, in whatever way is possible, other practices that help us to connect to the wisdom of fire are relational practices such as developing listening skills, practicing nonviolent communication, and transformative conflict resolution. These are all practices of healthy community, and it is a loving community that Jesus identifies as the signature manifestation of those who follow him (John 13:35).

When we engage with the Spirit of fire that lights our way—a guide for our unknown journey—we can relax into who we are and into our loving connection with reality. This is the path of love. It is the path of elemental wisdom; and now, having described these five elements, we can move to the final section, a discussion of how we live our lives in concert with creation's wisdom, even amid the great crises we are currently facing.

10

Living Elemental Practice

People facing threats they cannot defend themselves against—either because the threats are too large or because, as in the case of child abuse, the person is too small or weak to defend themselves or because the threatening habit is too powerful—are equipped with psychological tools to help them survive. Two of these tools are dissociation and denial. Dissociation is the process of thought that disconnects us from the body; we try to "go somewhere else," removing ourselves from what we are experiencing, which, as noted earlier, is a common response to a traumatic event. Denial is a retreat into the "ignoring" category of our ego process. We pretend that something harmful isn't happening. The process of substance abuse, where the addict refuses to admit their problem, is a classic example of this psychological mechanism. Both of these processes are at work in our individual and collective response to the climate crisis.

Because climate change is a global phenomenon, it seems too massive for any one person or community to address. I can get rid of my car, put solar panels on my house, eat less meat, insulate my home, turn the thermostat down, and the earth will continue to warm. This apparent powerlessness causes people to slip into a dissociative state in which we become disconnected from ourselves and from the environment.

For example, I was recently walking along a city street behind a young couple who, after unwrapping some snacks and cigarettes, mindlessly threw the wrappers on the ground as they ate and smoked. Not only were they doing something, smoking, that is harmful to themselves, they also seemed unconcerned that they were polluting the environment with their garbage. Their minds were disconnected from both their physical bodies and the body of the earth of which they are a part.

Denial is such a common response to climate change that we name an entire class of people "climate-change deniers." Most prominent in the United States, this group of millions of people simply try to wish away the reality of climate change by denying its existence.

These responses, again common human practices, often feel better than the anxiety that wells up in us when we try to face a problem we cannot fix. For those with trauma-related syndromes, dissociation can be more comfortable than the anxiety and pain caused by remembering the traumatic event. Similarly, because climate change causes anxiety, people struggle with whether to pay attention to the reality of what is happening to our world or, being overwhelmed by their powerlessness, simply "check out" and continue to go about their lives.

The Five Wisdom practice is ideally suited to overcoming the challenges of dissociation and denial as we engage a world struggling with the climate crisis. These teachings and the practice of relating directly to our elemental selves help us and our communities become fully embodied human beings working for good and healing in our troubled world. In this chapter we will outline the overall shape of living an elemental life of faith.

Inhabiting Space with Compassion and Loving Kindness

The Five Wisdom practice turns our awareness toward the reality of space. As discussed earlier, we are encouraged to pay attention to the three-dimensional world we inhabit and listen to the wisdom that exists within and without our embodied selves. Our knowledge of the atomic world is catching up to this ancient assertion regarding the nature of nonmaterial intelligence in the universe as we learn that wisdom and information are everywhere. Viruses and plasmids packed with information in the form of DNA and RNA move from one being to another, sharing this information even across species. The quantum phenomenon of "spooky action at a distance,"[1] in which two interacting particles can transmit information to each other across space and time, is now being used to manufacture our next generation of computers. The space around us is not inert; it is bubbling with intelligence and the Five Element Wisdom practice draws our attention to this reality.

Yet, rather than being open to the wisdom in the space we occupy, we relate to our experience from the ego perspective of *passion*, *aggression*, or *ignorance*. We aren't friendly to ourselves, and we judge all of our sensory input from the perspective of being right, wrong, or discarded.

From a very young age, this habit of judgment is reinforced as we're taught that everything we do is judged. We are given grades, standardized test scores, told when we are good and when we are bad, and most of our religious communities

---

1. For a very detailed discussion of this theorem, see "Bell's Theorem," in *Stanford Encyclopedia of Philosophy*, first published July 21, 2004; substantive revision March 13, 2019, www.plato.stanford. edu. Less rigorous discussions are widely available online.

emphasize judgment, some to a terrifying degree. Internalizing the judgmental behavior that's directed at us, we are soon able to direct it at ourselves from within. This is the negative self-talk that constantly plagues us, causing us to fear our very thoughts and feelings. As we cannot control what we think and feel, our minds become terrible overlords. In response, believing these judgments to be true, we become victims to these taskmasters, and our lives warp into a futile infinity of wasted energy as we try to please our internalized gods who are never satiated. This relationship with space is one that is claustrophobic, violent, and oppressive, and, when enacted on a societal scale, manifests all of the problems of our world.

The Five Wisdom practice invites us into a different relationship with space, a relationship of compassion and loving kindness. Such a relationship helps us overcome denial and dissociation. This approach recognizes that we are one of the voices in our heads! Our ability to be aware of the flow of our experience is a powerful tool helping us inhabit space lovingly. Instead of being afraid of our minds and ruthlessly judging ourselves, we can become curious about our experience without judgment. We do not need to fear a thought or a feeling, but, rather, we can engage our minds fearlessly.

This spiritual practice requires a safe space, a healing environment for the development of awareness, especially for those who have been abused in any way or those who come from marginalized or oppressed groups within their society. In the United States, this is particularly people of color but also those who are in gender minorities where there are many spaces in this world that are not safe and where certain thoughts or feelings, when expressed, can be dangerous. For example, the racist trope of the "angry black woman," common in the United States, is one that seeks to judge and oppress black women whenever they express legitimate anger at the racist systems and people against which they struggle.

While white people of privilege can take for granted that they can go on a spiritual retreat in a safe place to explore their minds, most people in the world cannot assume these spaces are available to them. For example, one evening, in the middle of a retreat where I was teaching, some of the white attendees were discussing a center in rural Missouri that they thought was a great place to go on retreat. The one African American at the table was silent during the conversation, but from the look on his face and from many conversations I've had with people of color, it wasn't a stretch to imagine his thoughts: An all-white space near a small town in rural Missouri isn't a safe place for a black man. Yet this reality didn't even occur to the white pastors around the table. These painful truths point to the necessity of intentionally creating safe spaces for all people to explore who they are, and when people from marginalized communities are involved, they must be given leadership roles in describing and creating these spaces based on their needs and experiences.

Once these safe spaces are created,[2] we become curious about our experience. "What are we noticing?" is the classic spiritual direction question. What do we notice about our internal experience, our external experience? Like a small child who has just learned to crawl, we begin to move about our environment, exploring it as if it were brand new. What habits and patterns do we notice in our minds? What does it tell us that we always think the same thoughts or have the same feelings about people no matter who they are? Why do we always assume that we are unlovable no matter what we are told by others?

These questions develop our awareness, something in short

---

2. Safe healing spaces can include therapy, spiritual direction, prayer groups, support and affinity groups, retreats, etc.

supply in our world, because compassion and loving kindness allow the artificial claustrophobia of the ego to dissolve. Not only do we notice our own ego patterns, but we notice the wisdom inherent in the world. If Wisdom does indeed meet us in every thought, then she is always there, always inviting us to understand ourselves and the world more deeply and fully. This stance of open awareness and loving compassion is central to the Five Wisdom approach, and indeed to all contemplative practices.

One technique used in elemental practice is "aimless wandering." When we wish to spend time with a particular element, such as earth, we allow ourselves to wander on the earth, walking, sitting, lying down, but all the while having a spirit of openness and watchfulness. What do we see, feel, smell? What thoughts come to mind? What bodily sensations do we experience? This practice allows us to notice both the wisdom and neurotic aspects of the element and brings us into a place of vast spaciousness. With this basic approach in mind, let's now review the embodied experience of the elements and see how a relationship of compassion can open the possibility of choosing wisdom over neurosis.

The Embodied Elemental Experience

As noted above, each element and energy has a particular relationship with one of our body's organs. In Chinese and Tibetan medicine, these relationships are explained and described in detail and form the basis for those cultures' systems of healing. My intention here is to provide a basic framework that helps our elemental relationships and allows us to become more aware of, and present to, wisdom.

When we breathe, we engage the space element directly. Our body expands, takes up more space as the space that was outside of us enters us. In the chapter on space, we noted the relationship between the lungs and the space element, and how breathing and drawing our attention to the breath can help us focus on space, moving us from claustrophobia to spaciousness. The development of this open awareness can be a regular practice.

As you move about your day, notice the space around you and that you are in space. How do you relate to space? Do you hold your breath in fear? Are you open to the wisdom of vast space, becoming a vessel for equanimity and peace? What allows you to feel safe in space? Where are the dull, ignoring edges of your mind? A helpful practice to engage space is to visualize the entire range of space in the universe, from the smallest nucleus of an atom to the largest galaxies in the universe,[3] realizing that each of us is a part of this vast array of space and spaces. Rest in this truth. Breathe.

The awareness of inner personal space moves out into a social and collective awareness of space. Perhaps you are drawn to understand more about how the space in your community is used. Is there open space where people can interact with the nonhuman natural world? Is there affordable housing space? How does your community deal with people who have been given no space to exist?

Or you might become more aware of the collective spaces you inhabit. The discipline of *feng shui* (pronounced "fung shway") is the Chinese art of spatial arrangement that endeavors to design furniture layouts that are harmonious and healthy. Do the rooms in your house feel open and hospitable or are they claustrophobic? How do you feel when you enter different spaces such as your office, your home, or your friends'

---

3. A wonderful video of this visualization can be found at https://www.youtube.com/watch?v=EMLPJqeW78Q.

homes? Cultivate this attention to space. On the one hand, in a well-arranged and appointed space, we notice our bodies relax and we feel refreshed. On the other hand, spaces arranged in a cramped or confusing manner may increase our anxiety and inhibit our breathing.

As a retreat leader, I am always attending to the space of the retreat, how seating is arranged, how the room is set for sound and lighting, because these factors are important and helpful for the participants. Yet, frequently, I am made aware of the lack of attention given to space; people are stuck in the neurotic relationship of ignoring spaces they inhabit. How often have you attended a talk with sun or bright light shining on the projection screen so you cannot see the slides or where the sound quality in the room is so poor that you cannot hear? How often are you staring at the back of the head of a person you are listening to during a discussion or question time? These are experiences of neurotic space, and as we become more aware of this element, we can work with our environments to bring greater wisdom to our world.

The water element is related to the kidney system, which makes sense, because the kidneys filter the water of our body, purifying the blood and removing ions that are unhelpful. In the United States, as people drink more soda, coffee, and other manufactured drink products, we have become aware of our chronic dehydration. Unfortunately, the modern solution to this problem is the creation of the multibillion-dollar plastic water bottle industry, which is now a significant source of pollution in our waters. These plastic bottles are full of nothing more than tap water, and yet they are marketed to an unaware population as a more "pure" water. This scenario, our lack of hydration and then our societal response to that condition, is a perfect example of a neurotic relationship to the wisdom of the water element; it lacks clarity about ourselves and an understanding of the world around us.

In contrast, greater clarity about ourselves and the world around us emerges as we draw our attention to our relationship with water. We interact with water all the time, when we cook, clean, eat, drink; and this gives us many opportunities to enter into the experience of mirror-like wisdom. There is a reason that so many love long baths and showers. These are direct experiences of the water element, in which our whole being engages the wisdom quality of water. Clarity feels good. When we are in the presence of wisdom we feel radiant and brilliant; and every time we connect to the water element, we are refreshed.

We can pay closer attention to our hydration and how we hydrate. Recently, a friend was talking about how she was developing painful and debilitating muscle cramps. Asked if she was drinking much water, she replied, "No, I hardly ever drink anything." Six months later, after becoming intentional about drinking water every day, the cramps were gone. People who start hydrating properly often describe a greater clarity of mind, and they feel better. They are like a plant coming back to life after a drought. The image of a deer panting for water as our soul thirsts for God is a powerful image of the wisdom of water and how we are brought to life through the clarity of this element.

Moving beyond ourselves, our attention to water is drawn to the waters of the world. All water is interconnected, and pollution in one place soon drifts everywhere. A superb example of water neurosis and lack of clarity was in the early days of industrialization, when humans decided that the way to get rid of waste was simply to dump it in a larger body of water. By the 1970s, environmentalists had developed the slogan that "dilution is not the solution to pollution." This represented growth and a greater clarity in our relationship with water.

Yet today, society still has not learned from our experience of pollution, and as we become aware of water and our relationship with it, we may be drawn to maintain our fresh waters. Perhaps you decide to advocate for clean water policies, or you might make changes in your water use and what you put down the drain. Do the people you vote for have a water platform, and how is your community working to maintain its waters? Again, our awareness of the elemental life moves us out from our health and wholeness into the wholeness and healing of our world.

Although our lungs bring air into our bodies, the air element is associated with our liver, the organ of bodily purification. In the Christian tradition, the air element is associated with the Holy Spirit, the one who gives pure life; and as we become attentive to air, we notice how our lives and actions move in concert with this Spirit, the Spirit of compassionate action.

With the recent dramatic rise in autoimmune disease, we are becoming more certain that a source of the significant toxic load on our bodies is the flood of synthetic organic molecules saturating our environment. These compounds, deriving from the chemical and plastics industries, mimic natural compounds, especially hormones, and trick our bodies into actions that are harmful. The liver system is in charge of detoxifying our body and ridding us of these intruders, but the load is often too large for us to handle. On a molecular level, this overload correlates with the spiritual challenge of discerning wise action: of the millions of actions available to us each day, which one of them is "of God"?

The wisdom of air draws us into greater awareness of how we relate to our environment and the air we breathe. What sorts of chemicals and cleaners do we use around the house? Do we overwhelm ourselves and our environments with scents and "air fresheners," which are nothing more than synthetic toxins? Can we become more curious about the nature and composition of the products we use that go on our bodies? The paradox of wise action is that it is often the simplest action, and we find this wisdom reflected in the physical realm: a dilute solution of vinegar and water is really the only household cleaner you need, and the myriad of toxic products found in most kitchen cabinets can be discarded.

The attention to air makes us more aware of how we spend our time. What do we really do during the day? Are our activities compassionate to ourselves and others, or are we running around like chickens with our heads cut off, running harder but doing less? Do we attend to our spiritual lives, and do we pay attention to what is life giving for us versus that which is toxic and death dealing? Are we forced to work multiple jobs at low wages just to make ends meet?

This awareness can extend to our actions on behalf of other people, the earth, and climate change. Can we pick one set of actions and changes that are life giving and healing for ourselves and our community? Maybe we advocate for a living wage, reasonable education costs, or workers' rights in general. When these actions are done from the perspective of air wisdom, we recognize that we are working in concert with the Spirit of Life, which is deeply satisfying. This experience of spiritual grounding is a balm for the anxiety of disconnection, and it can lead us to action that is both powerful and accepting of our limits as finite creatures in a vast universe.

Earth is connected to our gastrointestinal (GI) system. This is not surprising since the earth is the source of our food nourishment. The GI tract is another organ system that is open to the outside world, and through the digestive process we transform earthly substances into energy and the substance of our bodies. The medical profession is becoming increasingly aware of the power of the digestive process for health and also of the relationship between our bodies and the billions of bacteria that live in our GI tract. These little helpers are an integral part of healthy digestion; and, when this population is malnourished, poisoned, or depleted, our health suffers.

Drawing our attention to the earth element and its wisdom of abundance begins with attending to our relationship with food. We are becoming more aware of the harmful effects of our industrial food industry, which mirrors our harmful relationship with the earth. Read the label of almost any standard packaged food, and you will see a list of chemicals the vast majority of which aren't actual food items. As we flood ourselves with this toxic stew, our GI tract suffers and, as a result, so does our health. The standard American diet, which carries the appropriate acronym SAD, is an entry into the realm of the hungry ghosts. The more junk food we consume, the more hungry and ill we feel.[4]

In our globalized world, we have watched whole populations who were relatively healthy on a diet of real, indigenous food become ill when they were forced to move to a diet of processed foods either because of migration or because huge multinational corporations took over their food supply. In these trends, we see the neurotic relationship with the earth element.

Yet as we bring our attention to the earth we can heal these relationships. Not only can we learn to eat real foods, but we can work on relearning when we are actually hungry and eat out of need rather than habit. We can also work on our body image, which, particularly for women, is the focus of much abuse and unhealthy distortion.

---

4. The movie *Super Size Me*, which traces the experience of a man who eats nothing but junk food for thirty days, is a terrifying look at the effects of such food on the body.

These healing actions extend beyond ourselves. Perhaps we can become interested in our food system as a whole, involve ourselves with farmers' markets, or advocate for good food policy in our community. If we live in the United States, we may start questioning the cultural habit of the American lawn, a toxic waste dumping ground that simply reflects our deeply neurotic, controlling relationship with the earth. Maybe we will stop putting chemicals on our land and grow a garden or simply allow native plants to share space with us. Entering the realm of abundance, we will find ourselves wasting less, wanting less, and using less. This again is the paradox of the spiritual life: when we connect with the abundance of the Spirit, we crave less in the material world and our footprint on the earth becomes smaller.

Fire is the element of the heart, the seat of loving relationship. When God imagines the new future through the prophets, it is a future in which human beings know they are loved (see Isaiah 43:1–7). Awareness of the energy of fire is awareness of the nature of our relationships: with self, others, and God. As Jesus tells us, to manifest love within these relationships is the essence of the entirety of biblical teachings (see Matthew 22:36–40).

Yet, as we have noted, alienation—a lack of love—is central to the climate crisis. Throughout our human landscape, we see people treated as commodities rather than human beings. Whether it is in the realm of work, our intimate relationships, how we treat one another online, or the images we see on reality TV, there is a profound heartlessness that pervades our world. This is the neurotic relationship with fire; the power of love is turned into the power of incineration. Instead of compassion and kindness, we treat ourselves and one another as objects to be used and discarded. It is no wonder that people are increasingly isolated and report having fewer friends, less sex, and are lonelier.

Becoming aware of the energy of fire means being more nurturing and kind. We notice how we treat ourselves, how we create space for caring in our lives. Do we take the time to listen, to be deeply present to those in our lives, or are we tuned out? Many have pointed to scenes of crowds of people ignoring one another as they stare at their phones, and it is becoming more common to see parents ignoring their child's pleas while they check their email. This observation isn't to say that technology is all bad, but it's an invitation to consciously turn our attention and recognize when we are connecting with others and when we are simply tuning out.

Fire is also the element of community, which we address in more detail in chapter 12. For now, it is important to recognize that spiritual life and practice are not about individual spiritual achievement, but are done, rather, in and with others for the sake of the world. Becoming curious about our community experience, we look at how we nourish relationships in those communities, how are we making ourselves vulnerable and present, fanning the flames of connection and love.

Becoming aware of our heart connections, and how we tend to them, overcomes alienation, and the fundamental alienation of the human condition that Christians call the "fallen world." In Buddhism, it is the move beyond the ego self into the realm of enlightenment. This experience of the wisdom of fire brings with it a deep and abiding sense of the presence of the Spirit in our lives where we can meet both the joys and challenges of our world from a place of love.

Awareness Brings Choice

When we are living out of the habit and claustrophobia of ego, we are deluded in thinking that we make choices in our lives. Unfortunately, we are much more like the zombies of a horror film, wandering aimlessly, governed by our mindless desires, constantly repeating the same patterns of behavior, and in the process creating more zombies. The spiritual life, and the life of elemental wisdom, moves us into that spacious place where our awareness operates with freedom and true choice.

Practicing elemental awareness, we learn when we are in a neurotic relationship with a particular element, and when we move to the place of wisdom in relation to that same element. This flickering of mind happens naturally, and as we notice these shifts, we move from an ego-based relationship to one governed by the flow of the Spirit. As we recognize the quality of the elemental energy, we allow our minds to relax and move with the energy rather than trying to grasp or control it with our habitual patterns. We've all had these experiences, but usually we don't notice them or we do not understand what is happening to us. When I notice the vibrant autumnal colors of the trees, I sense the powerful earth energy and choose to be filled with its power or be lost and feel small because I don't believe this energy belongs to me. This is the movement from neurosis to wisdom.

Such true choice takes practice, the essence of the spiritual life. This chapter has presented an overview of the elemental life. One way we can focus our elemental practice is to examine our own particular elemental journey and focus on the one or two elements that are dominant in us as individuals. In understanding the energies most present within us, we become more aware of the movement from neurosis to wisdom. This movement clears the way for a life of greater choice and freedom, and by dwelling in that freedom, we experience the truth that God makes straight our paths in the wilderness (see Isaiah 42:16).

11

Tracing Your Elemental Journey

Returning to the image of Wisdom working beside God at the beginning of creation (Proverbs 8:22–31), we can imagine the wonderful alchemy of time and space that created the Big Bang. Light and energy explode onto the scene and set in motion the endless dance of particles and heat, of combining and dispersing. This elemental soup continues to expand and cool, producing stars, planets, galaxies. And all the while, Wisdom and God are designing, forming, destroying, merging, and dispersing the elements, and all of it is good. This process continues over a long human time frame, or a short theological time frame, and eventually earth is formed.

Following another period of time, humans come onto the scene, emerging from this long, beautiful dance of creation. From the perspective of the Five Elements teaching, the elements, endowed with the attributes of the Spirit of God, have been present throughout this process; and so the history of creation is the history of the elements, and that history is embodied within each being, within each of us.

Each distinct object in the universe is comprised of a unique combination of elements. In living systems, billions of pairs of DNA molecules sort themselves to form individuals that have never been and never will be again. From an elemental perspective, we might imagine that each DNA base pair is one "unit" of an element. In the same way that only four types of DNA molecules[1] can create billions of unique creatures, so too can five elements sort themselves into billions of unique beings. Each one of us is the result of trillions of moments of elemental play, and each one carries that history through life.

This vision of an elemental history connecting and forming each being on earth, both animate and inanimate, is far different from the individualistic, self-sufficient, alienated-from-the-rest-of-creation image that is handed to us by Western industrial society. It is a vision of connection and uniqueness and is the brilliance, the wisdom, of creation: we are all One, but we are also all our own expression of the master worker. When we look at the elemental expressions around us, we see that sometimes one element stands out clearly: the ocean is distinct from dry land; the flame of a fire is different from a cool breeze. Most of the time, however, the elements are combined, with some having more prominence than others.

Similarly, each person expresses one or two dominant elemental energies, just as seasons, cultures, and landscapes express a dominant energy; and understanding our dominant energy is a valuable use of the Five Elements system. In this manner, these teachings are somewhat like other personality systems, such as the Myers-Briggs Type Indicator or the Enneagram. However, note that the Five Elements teaching isn't about labeling oneself or others with a particular "type" or solid diagnosis. Rather, awareness of our elemental makeup is an aspect of our contemplative practice and aids in developing our capacity to move from a neurotic experience to one of wisdom.

---

1. DNA is made up of two strings of four base molecules paired with one another: adenine (A), thymine (T), guanine (G), and cytosine (C).

Awareness of Our Elemental Makeup

Developing familiarity with the manifestations of the Five Elements, we notice the dominant energies in our life. Examining our experience, we can ask: What elements am I naturally drawn to? How do I act and feel when I am stressed, and how does this reflect a particular neurotic experience? What are the things I love to do, and how do these relate to one of the elements? Starting this exploration, you may realize that you have always loved being near water or that your house is richly decorated. You may enjoy "moving all the time," or perhaps you feel most alive when you are relating to your many friends. These observations hint at your dominant energy.

Developing our felt sense of each elemental energy, we also cultivate awareness of our energetic makeup. By spending time with each element, we recognize the full gestalt of that energetic experience. We have a bodily experience of the solidity of earth, the warm exciting nurture of fire, the light movement of air, the clear nourishment of water, and the still vastness of space. These experiences help us to recognize our dominant experience, and we notice the familiar flow of wisdom and neurosis that has been with us for our entire life. Such self-awareness moves out into an awareness of wisdom, of the divine Spirit who is present within each of these energies; and, in turn, this greater awareness allows for an experience of healing as we choose to align our being with wisdom.

Engaging this elemental journey of awareness also connects us with the wounds and traumas of both our individual lives, and also the collective inherited life of which we are the present manifestation. This encounter with our woundedness highlights the need for compassion and loving kindness on our elemental journey. Often when we encounter the habitual patterns of our ego, many of which are formed in reaction to these traumas, we want to be rid of them, and this impulse results in significant aggression toward ourselves—the famous "beating ourselves up." From the perspective of the Five Elements, this is a neurotic expression of water: the clarity generated by our awareness turns to aggressive judgment and rejection.

When we address our habits in this manner, however, they only grow stronger and more intractable. In contrast, when we enter a safe space where we can direct kindness toward ourselves and allow the habit to be revealed for what it is, empty and without permanent power, we can watch it dissolve and be replaced by love and wisdom. This transformation through loving awareness is at the heart of the spiritual journey, and its value is increasingly recognized by a variety of healing modalities.[2]

We also cultivate our elemental journey when we come to understand our history and the particular cultures, geographies, and indigenous backgrounds from which we have been formed. Such an exploration also connects us with the historical traumas that have been foisted on our ancestors, often aided by oppressive religious structures. At this point in human history, most of the world's population has, in some way, been shaped by the rise of global colonialism, which began in the fifteenth century and has continued through the Age of Industrialization into the new era of globalization. Identifying our place within this history teaches us about the pain and trauma that we carry in our bodies and our consciousness. These collective wounds also help form the neurotic reactions to our elemental makeup.

For example, in the United States, people of color, particularly the black and Native American populations, suffer various health-related problems at greatly elevated rates compared to the white population. These illnesses are not the result of a dif-

---

2. These include, but are not limited to, mindfulness-based psychotherapy and psychedelic-assisted psychotherapy.

ference in the physiology of these populations, as is sometimes thought by a medical profession dominated by unconscious racism, but, rather, they result from historical trauma, the trauma of slavery, dislocation, genocide, racism, and cultural obliteration. Members of these communities are recognizing that reconnecting with their indigenous roots, with their ancient wisdoms, most of which have some type of elemental wisdom at the heart of their teachings, helps to heal these wounds.

For those who are in the oppressive classes or groups, it may appear that our lives are "fine," but we—and I am a member of such a group as a white American male—are also deeply wounded and disconnected from wisdom as a result of our journey of trauma. The creation of "white people" in the Virginia colony in the 1620s, which we alluded to earlier, was the beginning of a four-hundred-year bargain with the devil for those who entered that social group. In exchange for a myriad of economic, political, and social privileges, our basic humanity was suppressed as we agreed to be part of one of the great exploitations in human history.

The collective denial of the pain this deal created, and continues to create, is a perfect example of space neurosis: ignoring the trauma enacted on others within the space we collectively inhabit. One can see this pain erupt whenever white people are confronted with the reality of racism. The label "white fragility"[3] refers to the defensive reactions of white people when they are faced with critiques of racism. This is a classic space and water neurosis reaction. When a person is faced with an opportunity to wake up from their ignoring state, they fiercely try to go back to sleep through a combination of aggressive rejection and deflective denial.

---

3. See Robin DiAngelo, *White Fragility: Why It's So Hard for White People to Talk about Racism* (Boston, MA: Beacon Press, 2018).

Another example of the manifestation of historical trauma is found in populations that have come to live near areas of massive environmental destruction. In the Appalachian region of the United States, coal mining has turned to ever more destructive techniques for coal extraction, the latest being mountaintop removal. People who live near these sites of environmental catastrophe have a life expectancy of up to a dozen years lower than the national average and rates of illness many times that of the rest of the population.

These experiences crush the spirits of the people in this region, and the rates of displacement, opioid addiction, spousal abuse, and a variety of mental health problems are sky high. This type of human and social catastrophe can be found around the world anywhere that environmental destruction is taking place, and the long-term results of this is a disconnection from the wisdom inherent in the elemental world and thus from God.

Engaging our elemental journey means grappling with these experiences that have, in one manner or another, formed each of us. Consequently, with the elemental energies at play and our ego habits in relation to them, as well as the traumas that have formed the habits, we can compassionately allow ourselves to be open to Wisdom, who heals our wounds and returns us to the wisdom of our indigenous roots.[4]

Entering Wisdom's House

Embarking on our elemental journey is to enter wisdom's house, an activity and image central to healthy religious and spiritual

---

4. Unfortunately, some of the white power, neo-Nazi groups are using this idea of indigenous roots as a way of recruiting white people, mostly young men, into their movements. This is a perversion of the reflections I am encouraging that lead to equality, justice, and tolerance.

practice. Unfortunately, religion is often what prevents and disconnects us from this life-giving endeavor. In the Gospel stories that describe Jesus as a healer, we see him spitting (Mark 7:33), making mud to put on a person's eyes (John 9:6), speaking to demons (Luke 4:41), and drawing on the ground with his finger (John 8:6). Today, we recognize and associate these activities with ancient healing practices and traditional healers.[5] They are the actions of a spiritual master who is deeply connected with the wisdom of God, which is present and working in the natural world.

Yet, as Christianity evolved and became increasingly identified with an empire, its theology developed, and it pulled away from nature, resulting in the loss of these obvious indigenous roots. Furthermore, when Christianity encountered other indigenous cultures and people, rather than seeing them as natural allies of the faith, it persecuted them, forcing them to give up and renounce their languages, cultures, and religions.

The Five Elements teachings help us to reconnect to these powerful elemental roots and recreate a faith system that values our inherent connection with the rest of creation. This is the role of healthy spiritual systems. By becoming aware of our primary energies and developing our practice of inhabiting the wisdom aspect of this energy, we too can become agents of change and healing.

If our dominant element is space, we recognize that we bring the presence of this loving container with us into any situation. We can offer acceptance and room for exploration to ourselves and others. People who have this as a dominant energy are often

---

5. Sometime these activities are referred to, particularly in certain Western spiritual circles, as "shamanic." This term, however, has numerous issues associated with cultural appropriation, which is why I prefer not to use it.

those at the table who rarely speak, but when they do share, they offer something of great value. These are the people who can be steady optimists in the face of challenge or who are good leaders by virtue of their ability to bring out the best in others; they are the strong silent types.

If our dominant element is earth, we love to feed and nourish others. Such people delight in the abundance that they bring to spaces they inhabit. Their energy overflows with creative possibilities, and they see the good in almost any situation. People who resonate with the earth can be great party planners and hosts and are most hospitable. With this energy there is always room at the table and always space on a lap for another child.

Reflecting the clarity of water, people with this primary energy bring vision and direction to groups or situations. These people see patterns in chaotic data or activity, and they can guide and lead groups and others toward deeper insights. Bringing mirror-like wisdom can catalyze positive movement toward a valuable goal or bring calm to anxious confusion. To provide a drink of water to the thirsty is a deeply loving act.

In a society full of phrenetic action, those who manifest the wisdom of air have the ability to do just what needs to be done, when it is the most useful. Such a person can help create activities that are satisfying, elegant, meaningful, and purposeful. If you have this as your dominant energy, you delight in "getting things done" in ways that are fun, playful, and decrease stress. Cultivating this wisdom helps others to realize the value of both action and stillness, for we love both a nice breeze and a still evening sunset.

Those who bring the heart energy of fire spread loving kindness everywhere. If this is your dominant quality you become aware of your gifts of kindness and compassion. People in the helping and healing professions are often fire-element people, and they radiate a warmth that others find deeply satisfying. This energy also helps with group cohesion, bonding, and networking. As you engage with your fire energy, you can see how you connect with others and create social spaces where good work can happen.

COMBINING ELEMENTAL ENERGIES

In the Jewish Passover liturgy, there is an interesting moment when those gathered at the table are called to "combine the elements." This involves mixing foods that represent both the bitterness of slavery and the sweetness of freedom. It is a ritual moment that recognizes the multilayered, multifaceted nature of our experience. In the Five Elements system, this combining of elements is also recognized as an essential aspect of life and health.

Despite having a general dominant energy, all the elements are present in our bodies; and, as noted earlier, illness is understood as a manifestation of an imbalance of the elements. Thus, in our lives and our communities, we are always seeking to balance our dominant elemental expression with the other elements, for we instinctively realize that balance is needed to create wholeness. If we have a very dominant fire quality, then water helps us become clearer about our heart's desires. If we are too grounded on the earth, a little air can help us move and become more relaxed and creative. The expression "opposites attract" speaks to our instinctive desire to balance energies.

Paul, in his discussion of the parts of the body (1 Corinthians 12:12–26) and the value of each part, was speaking to this need for balance and integration. In any organization, if we have too many leader types, the organization can flounder.

Similarly, if we do not appreciate those who work for an hourly wage, we can develop unjust, exploitative systems. Wisdom is found in all the elements. Unfortunately, the human ego has difficulty with this egalitarian concept. I'm sure Paul recognized that ego systems and structures value the head more than the toe. This is another expression of our fallen world and a source of great suffering.

Attending to the need for balance and cultivating an appreciation of all five energies can encourage us to venture outside of ourselves and appreciate, rather than fear, others. What if we understood that every culture and country was simply a particular expression of a dominant energy, and we realized that humanity's best hope for health and flourishing was to value and incorporate every expression of wisdom? The rainbow flag, a popular symbol for acceptance and equality, symbolizes this elemental whole. The billions of dollars we spend on weapons every year represents our projected fear of the other—the elemental expression we do not understand. Befriending the elements is also a practice within wisdom's house, and encouraging oneself and others in this task is a concrete activity we can undertake to promote world healing.

As we do this work of energetic, elemental connection, we recognize and remember that embracing wisdom for ourselves isn't a selfish act. Rather, in appreciating the gifts of wisdom, we find the truth in Jesus's teaching that love of self, other, and God is deeply interwoven; one is impossible without the other. In finding life for ourselves, we naturally share life with others. Living in wisdom's house brings joy both to us and to the rest of the world. Living from this place of inherent wisdom also helps us to recognize that we can live in this time of crisis as powerful people of faith. We recognize that we are fully a part of the natural world, and we choose actions and a state of being that is loving and fruitful even if we cannot immediately see any global changes resulting from our lives. In theological language, the Christian spiritual life describes this stance as that of a disciple, a term that we will now examine from the perspective of an elemental faith.

12

On Being Prepared for Anything

The original name for Christianity was "the Way" (Acts 9:2), a name that referred to a new community of people dedicated to following the way of Jesus. In this very early version of the Christian faith, the formation of a spiritual community was dedicated to the teachings and practices laid out by a spiritual teacher. Such community formation is common across many religious traditions, and the students in these communities are often called "disciples," a word that comes from the Latin term *discipulus*, which means one who is "a learner." The history of any spiritual tradition is the history of its spiritual teaching. How, in a particular time and place, do people learn to follow the Way? How do we engage deeply in the challenges of our time, mining our experience for wisdom and seeking the path of insight?

The movie *K-PAX* is a science-fiction film that offers a wonderful portrayal of Jesus, even though the film never mentions Jesus or Christianity. The plot revolves around an alien, Prot (pronounced *Prōt*), who appears in Grand Central Station in New York and immediately finds himself arrested and put in a psychiatric hospital, where he is always completely honest about his alien nature and his travels to earth. While interned as a patient, the relationships he forms with his fellow patients and the medical staff are conditioned by their relative power in the hospital system and their own ego states. The staff, who believe they are wise and are the powerful ones in the medical world, of course, think he is simply insane; and this assessment is mostly immune to the mounting evidence, which is presented as the story unfolds, that he is not a "normal" human being. To them, he is lovingly challenging and also dismissive of their claims to power over him, power they clearly do not have and which he demonstrates one day by disappearing and going to Greenland. When he returns to find the staff enraged by his disappearance, he calmly reminds them he had told them of this upcoming trip, information they, of course, disbelieved.

The patients, who are powerless within the medical system and whose egos have been largely shattered by their trauma, illness, and oppression within the psychiatric world, immediately believe his claims and can clearly see that he is very different from them. Prot relates to these people in a loving, gentle, and compassionate manner and begins to heal them, a fact that infuriates the doctors, who sense their nicely ordered hospital system, which benefits them more than it does the patients, spinning out of control.

Several of the patients and eventually one psychiatrist become Prot's "disciples," a term not used in the film but appropriate, for they begin to learn from him and follow his instructions, which are designed to heal them. As the movie unfolds, Prot makes it known that he is going to return to *K-PAX* (his planet, whose name poetically means *peace*) and that he is only going to bring one patient with him. The other disciples, like Jesus's original disciples, are charged with remaining on earth to be prepared for whatever comes their way. While it is clear that their work and life will not change the world, will not change the way psychiatric care is provided, and will seem fairly insignificant in the big scheme of things, it will nonetheless be important work; and their lives, and the world, will be better for it.

This has always been the nature of discipleship. While we may desire that the world as a whole be transformed and be a better place, individuals and groups do not have the power to enact such changes. What we can do is focus our minds, hearts, and lives on our spiritual paths so that we may confront whatever comes with love and compassion. This perspective on discipleship is particularly important today as we face the reality of the climate crisis.

FACING EXTINCTION

The climate crisis is causing us to face the possibility of the extinction of our species. This is the most terrifying aspect of the crisis. Although we know that millions of other species have come and gone throughout the history of the earth, as discussed earlier, modern humans have never seriously considered that extinction might happen to them. Again, such denial reflects an attitude that we are not really part of "nature" and that we are somehow special and immune to vicissitudes of change and the endless dance of matter and energy that defines the universe. But we are not, and the climate crisis appears to have penetrated this denial and confronted our collective mortality. How can the elemental perspective help with our paralysis and hopelessness?

We know that the universe is a vast interplay of time and space within which form and formlessness continue to unfold. In this system, nothing is lost. Information and connection are always conserved in some form or another even as these forms may shift dramatically. In the Buddhist tradition, it is said that at death our elements disperse and serve to create whatever beings or nonbeings come next. This conforms to what we know scientifically. In the Christian tradition, God is the holder of time and space and is always working to form and reform the universe, creating new events and providing people—new teachers and prophets—to help reorient them to the divine will. This experience of "continual unfolding" is captured in the notion of the eternal covenant: throughout history, God is always working with people, not giving up on them, trying to help them live lives of goodness and love. The elements have dispersed and reformed hundreds of times over the centuries, but God holds the thread of wisdom that weaves its way through the universe.

In an alienated state and in an alienated faith, our ego selves disconnect from this endless flow, and we are only interested in self-preservation. While this may feel good when our life goes according to our plans, when things fall apart and we are faced with our smallness and powerlessness, we panic. The powerful doctors in *K-PAX* are symbolic of this ego drive toward the delusion of wisdom, power, and control. The life of spiritual practice, however, encourages the dissolution of the ego self and the experience of our true and deep connection with the divine spirit of wisdom. The patients in the mental hospital, like the lepers and other ill and powerless people in the Gospel stories, have had their ego states destroyed by the traumas of the fallen human world, so they are more open to receiving the blessing that comes from connecting with God. They are hungry for grace, for elemental wisdom.

Working with our elemental practice, we slowly move from the neurosis of separation to the wisdom of connection. We experience the infinite flow of the elements of which we have always been a part. This is our connection to the ancestors—in Christianity, the communion of saints—and to our deep, deep roots as a common species sharing a common reality. In the Christian tradition, this connection is what we refer to as infinity; the information that comprises who we are is now part of the fabric of reality, and it continues forever.

Elemental spiritual practice, the practice of connecting to wisdom, makes this truth not just intellectual but experiential. This is what is meant by an embodied spirituality; we know in our bones, in our hearts, in our felt experience of reality that we are deeply connected to everything. This is profoundly nurturing, satisfying, and empowering. In the Buddhist tradition, the experience of our practice and of our connection to enlightened reality creates "primordial confidence." In experiencing the deep and abiding love that is the interconnection of all things, we become confident; we know that we are okay for now, and for eternity. We become the disciple that can stay on earth and face whatever happens. Elemental practice turns our fear and anxiety, as we face the possibility of human extinction, into fearlessness; and it can also focus our actions and efforts as we recognize that we do not have to worry about whether our actions are large or small.

Helpful for our work at this time of great transition is returning to our friends, the dinosaurs, and imagining the transition between their age of planetary dominance and the new age of mammals. The arising new, tiny species are the future of the earth, but, of course, that's not something they think about or realize. The giant dinosaurs are headed for oblivion and the movie screen, but they are still hugely powerful and can easily eat or crush the newly forming mammalian life. The mammals, as the new change that is coming, could try to engage the dinosaurs and directly "defeat" them, but this would be futile and a waste of their time. Instead, they work at surviving and creating the new way of being on earth that will ultimately flourish. Spiritual leaders have certainly spent time calling out and working for justice against large systems of oppression, and this is work to which some are called. But they have also emphasized that such work cannot be done at the expense of the deep spiritual work of growth and union with God. This goal of spiritual life, which appears small and irrelevant from the perspective of the powerful human ego structures, is the work of the small mammals: create a new path, a new way, and a way of wisdom.

ACTING FROM A PLACE OF FEARLESSNESS

To act from this place of wise fearlessness is to be aligned with our elemental wisdoms. Understanding and experiencing our dominant wisdom energies, and living from a place of wisdom versus a place of neurosis, we impart wisdom to the rest of the world regardless of our actions and the size or scope of our activity. If our dominant element is earth, we can bring abundance to any situation; air brings the gift of compassionate action; water provides clarity and insight; fire can help develop loving relationships; and space offers the equanimity of a wise space where everyone is welcome. These acts of wisdom create concrete and tangible good in the world that we inhabit, and which is always part of the wider world.

As we have the embodied experience of our deep and abiding place in the natural world, we realize that when we bring the wisdom of God into our lives, we also help to transform the embodied reality of the cosmos because everything is interconnected. We may not see the overall result or be convinced that we have enacted any change, yet we start to recognize that these issues are the concerns of the ego self; as is a nihilism that results in an attitude of "I can't make a big difference, so I'll do nothing." Entering wisdom's house, an act that happens any time a wisdom element is revealed, is enough for us for now. This is what we can do, and we experience that moment as a whole and holy moment. Such an experience alleviates our anxiety and frees us to continue in fearlessness.

These holy moments highlight the connecting power of a fearless life lived from the perspective of the wisdom energies. Christianity has always proclaimed that the disciples of Jesus are connected with God as a branch is connected to a vine (see John 15:5). Yet, unfortunately, many people who claim Christianity as their faith do not experience this connection. As we have seen throughout the description of the elemental perspective, such a view and practice help us to connect deeply with everything around and in us. Living out of such a connection inspires great compassion and concern for the rest of reality, and this concern, which is grounded and powerful not anxious and weak, draws our attention toward our outward life.

This movement from inner life to outer life is the natural movement of the Spirit and has always inspired individuals and communities to work for good in the world. The more we live from fearlessness, the more we are freed to respond to the crisis of our time in life-giving ways. Wisdom leads and guides us into new modes of being, and as our awareness of spiritual, elemental space deepens, our experience of three-dimensional reality changes.

For many people, the body is an autonomous vehicle for transporting our heads, and the world is a solid, material space full of objects. This is the disembodied, alienated state we've explored throughout this book. Often, we notice our body only when something goes wrong with it, when we stub our toe or need food or sex. Objects in the world feel flat and hard, and even animate objects and creatures are there just for our use or annoyance. As we become aware of elemental energies and the presence of wisdom, this view changes. Our experience of ourselves becomes more alive and integrated, and the experience of our external reality also shifts. Rather than solid objects, we now recognize embodied spiritual entities; we can feel the abundance, the flow, the clarity, the heart, and the spaciousness of creation. Now our lives and our actions open into the wider world of God's reality—the cosmic dance of creation.

This awareness awakens us to new possibilities for self-care and reflection as well as action in the world. An acquaintance, whose dominant energy is water, upon learning about the elemental system, realized why they spontaneously ran to get in the shower when they had a panic attack. Being close to the element was incredibly calming and soothing, although at the time they didn't know why. Another person, who manifests earth, lit up realizing how in times of stress they always wanted to go for a walk at night. Furthermore, they didn't know why they liked the yellow room in their house, but recognized that it just "felt good." Entering the realm of wisdom can allow us to be more intentional as we navigate our reality, rejoicing in the presence of elemental Wisdom and listening for her call to insight.

Following her lead, our lives become richer, joy-filled, and focused. Perhaps we are led to join an organization that works for clean energy use; maybe we are more focused on changing our lifestyle, the way we eat, the way we travel, where we live; maybe we are drawn toward working for justice in a particular area of life and society. While these activities can be done with or without a particular sense of spirituality, when they are combined with the elemental perspective, we experience them in a new way; they are filled with the light and life of the Spirit versus being just another task on our "to-do list."

Moving outward with confidence and wisdom is not something we are called to do alone. All spiritual movements, and particularly Christian spirituality, have asserted that our spiritual lives are to be lived in community. This community focus mirrors the interconnectedness of life and the communal nature of biological systems. Just as the wisdom energies and elements combine to form our experience of the world, so we are called to manifest interconnection and form communities who pray together, work together, and support life together. The destruction of community by our alienated culture, with its focus on individualism, is, as I've mentioned, one of the major causes of the crises we face.[1]

The elemental spiritual approach can encourage us to seek out this vital community life and help us to feel a sense of mutual support as we face these crises together. We begin to understand how we gravitate toward people with different elemental energies to balance our own or how we align with communities whose particular gifts, skills, or approach match our primary energies. Many of the most innovative ways of living in our time of climate change focus on our communal existence. From the building of tiny house communities to a focus on sharing resources, the more we intentionally cultivate ways of living that are wise, the more we will find the solutions that enliven and empower us.

Finally, living fearlessly allows us to enter the suffering of the world. This has always been an essential aspect of the spiritual life in general and the Christian spiritual life, in particular, but it is one that has fallen out of favor, especially in the United States, where more "Christians" believe that Christianity is only about receiving God's favor and a bigger house.[2] Attention to

---

1. For an outstanding discussion of the opioid epidemic and its roots in the destruction of community, see Sam Quinones, *Dreamland: The True Tale of America's Opiate Epidemic* (New York: Bloomsbury Press, 2015).

2. The so called "prosperity gospel" is the worst offender here, but increasingly the entire fundamentalist movement in the United States has been trending in these directions.

elemental wisdom can also help us to face suffering bravely, a task that is connected to the healing of our traumas.

FEARLESSLY ENGAGING OUR WOUNDS

Entering the suffering of the world first requires that we can enter into our own suffering. We have noted how, when we enter our mind—when we engage our spiritual journey—the first person we always encounter is ourselves. In other words, we confront our neuroses, our wounds, our fears, our ego, and this encounter is challenging. An embodied practice, such as the Five Elements teaching, reveals the trauma responses that are lodged in our bodies and the need to find environments that can heal us from these past hurts.

Unfortunately, such environments are hard to find. In the United States, three out of five people suffering from mental and emotional pain cannot get help. In other parts of the world, the percentage is much higher. Churches, communities that are the legacy of Jesus who walked the streets dispensing free medical care, are sadly lacking in their response to people's pain. What if every church building, no matter how many worshiped there on Sunday, was a center for holistic healing? What if these were places of safety where we could gather and engage our trauma and heal without judgment?

The call of wisdom is and always has been to create such spaces and is an essential aspect of the elemental work and that of the spiritual life, in general. We cannot heal from suffering if we are on our own, with no safety and no community. But once we can enter such a space—such as therapy, nonmedical or holistic healthcare practitioners such as body workers and acupuncturists, spiritual direction, support groups, retreats, and prayer circles—we can enter our embodied experience and release the traumas that are placeholders for our suffering.

The central Christian story, the story of Jesus, is a story of entering the suffering of the world. God takes on this suffering for the purpose of transformation. As Jesus encountered those who were suffering in his time, he healed them as a sign of God's presence and God's desire for a world that is free of pain. The resurrection is the ultimate act of God's power, an indication that even as matter and energy are continually transformed, the love and presence of God is always there, always working for life. Yet the crucifixion tells us that we cannot get to this place of eternity by avoiding the suffering of the world. The desire to run from suffering is the activity of the ego, which is always trying to avoid distress and fortify itself against death. In contrast, Jesus shows us that it is only by engaging the suffering of the world and entering the reality of suffering that we can emerge whole.

Our elemental practice and other healing practices help us to walk through the cauldron of transforming fire and be reborn as our true selves, the image of God within us revealed in the light of wisdom. This is the path of fearlessness and it prepares us for whatever comes our way.

13

Conclusion:
Listening to Wisdom's Call

The television series *Mars*, produced by National Geographic, is a brilliant portrait of the issues facing us today. The series takes a unique approach, combining current-day scientific facts regarding the issues of climate change and exploration to Mars with science fiction as it portrays what Mars exploration will look like starting in 2033. Among the many subplots of the show, a thread that emerges is that—without any personal and collective change in the state of our being—what we do on Mars will simply be a replication of what we are currently doing on Earth.

What the show doesn't discuss explicitly is the "why" of this repetition of habitual patterns. Although it lays significant blame at the feet of large multinational corporations, a reasonable place to lay blame, it doesn't recognize that the seeds of "business as usual" are present from the start of the Mars mission. The people sent to the planet are brilliant scientists, but they seem fairly devoid of deeper spiritual wisdom. They regularly try to ignore their feelings; they have poor relationship skills; and they immediately get into power struggles with one another and the different missions that arrive on the planet. Clan violence is obviously just around the corner. The narrators in the present-day segments of the show, again all brilliant and accomplished scientists and people, do not understand that the corporate ego that haunts our time is just a systemic, large organizational ego structure that has arisen out of the conglomeration of millions of individual egos.[1]

These narrators hint that our human approach to the world must change if a Mars colony is going to be any different from life on Earth, but all they have to offer are vague ideas about "international cooperation" and "prioritizing science" over profit. This book is an attempt to be more explicit in describing that different approach. The only way for human society to have a different outcome in the future, whether it is on this planet, another one, or within the world of virtual reality, is to develop a fundamentally different relationship with ourselves, the world, and others.

This book presents illustrations and biblical images of these new relationships, one of which is the inversion of common social hierarchies. For example, in the parable of the laborers, Jesus talks about the first being last and the last being first (see Matthew 20:1–15); Mary says that those of low degree will be exalted and the mighty will be brought down (Luke 1:52), and the prophets describe the destruction of kings and justice for the poor. These inversions are symbolic of the overthrow of the human ego and the establishment of divine wisdom within human society.

Sadly, however, even the church promotes the same hierarchical structures as other human imperial structures: the higher in the church hierarchy you rise, the more money you make, and the more status and power you have. What greater evidence do we need of the power of the ego process than the blindness of these human organizations to the teachings within their found-

---

1. For an outstanding description of the corporate ego process, see William Stringfellow, *An Ethic for Christians and Other Aliens in a Strange Land* (Eugene, OR: Wipf & Stock, 2004 [rept. ed.]).

ing documents? Imagine if bishops made less than starting pastors. If you wish to watch the aggression of the human ego at work, try getting that legislation passed within your church organization.

The image of hierarchical inversion also points to possibly the most essential tool for the spiritual life—humility. Humility arises in each of us as we recognize our position in nature as creatures and not the creator, the position our ego would like to occupy. In the wisdom tradition, this distinction is manifest in the instruction that the "fear of the LORD is the beginning of wisdom" (Proverbs 9:10). Unfortunately, like many potentially helpful spiritual instructions, the phrase "fear of the LORD" may almost be unusable because it has been fashioned as a weapon in so many church settings, causing fear and trauma. If this is your experience, perhaps substituting the word "respect" or "recognition" might be better.

In modern scientific language, this phrase would be akin to saying that you cannot ignore the laws of nature. The climate crisis is teaching us this hard truth. If we turn the earth into a heat trap, it will burn whether we like it or not. Recognizing that we are subject to these laws is humbling, and developing humility is what the wisdom tradition wishes for us. Humility places us on the spiritual path, moving from the neurosis of the ego to the wisdom of enlightenment.

The wisdom tradition also develops the notion of laws of nature, which in the ancient world were called God's commandments; and following God's commandments is the second basic instruction we follow to become wise. In the series *Mars*, the narrators, as they struggle to explain the difference between the common human approach and formulating a new approach, frequently mention the idea of putting people before money. This phrase is a good shorthand description of following God's commandments, which, as we know, are distilled in the law of love—loving God, neighbor, and self. Of course, love, true love, places people first and makes us willing to sacrifice for others, including the entire creation.

The beauty of the elemental approach to our spiritual lives is that it gives us numerous concrete ways daily to practice choosing love, choosing wisdom, choosing to give up our ego selves. We are in direct contact with the basic elements every second of our being. God isn't somewhere far away, but right here and now; and wisdom is calling us to pay attention and follow into the future. This is the essence of listening to wisdom's call.

This future orientation needs to be explicit because environmentalism is often described in the language of preservation, a term used frequently throughout the *Mars* series. Hopefully, it is clear from earlier discussions that preservation of some moment in time, some ecological condition, is impossible. I can no more freeze a forest in time than I can freeze my age at twenty-five. The environmental preservation movement is often, rightly, criticized as an elitist approach—resulting in the exclusion of many who cannot afford the expensive equipment or travel to get to the preserved places—for the benefit of the few. Furthermore, preservation often can sound like "anti-progress," and the pejorative term "Luddite" was coined to denote this idea.

The Five Wisdom approach, like the spiritual life in general, is neutral with respect to any particular set of material conditions. This is the state of spiritual indifference cultivated by a life of prayer. Wisdom can be found in the woods, in a cave, in a stone church, or in a glass skyscraper. It can be found in oral language, in written language, and in computer code. In each era, as things change and progress, a favorite human pastime, usually monopolized by the older generation, is to blame the new things that appear for the problems of the world. Today, technology is often the focus of such complaints. But this approach is faulty and misses the point. The problem isn't outside of us; it's within us. It is the ego process. When we understand this, we realize that each new moment, with its new technology, is just another combination of the elements, a new manifestation of creation in which wisdom delights. The issue isn't whether or not technology is good or bad, the issue is: How can we engage technology from a wisdom perspective? Elemental practice can help us find the answer to this question and to the more general question: How can you be wise in your daily living?

The COVID-19 pandemic is pushing us to ask how we can live wisely in an unprecedented manner. Such an event makes the content of this work even more relevant and urgent. As I write, I am, like most of humanity, staying isolated; my life has changed dramatically in a few short weeks. While this is a terrible event, it is also an opportunity to re-evaluate how we function as a species. For years, people have been saying that our current way of life is unsustainable, yet we have generally gone on living as before. Now, amid this pandemic, with planes grounded, people isolated, commerce grinding to a halt, and our food systems at risk, we are experiencing what it means to be forced—by the ecological systems we are a part of—to live differently. Elemental spiritual practice, listening to Wisdom and learning her ways, can help us; but we need to take her call seriously.

When I lead a retreat or give a series of talks, I end my last presentation with the encouragement "Practice your faith." This is my encouragement to you: practice wisdom; practice moving from neurosis to wisdom; practice being humble; practice seeking the Spirit of God in your elemental nature and the elemental nature around you; practice love and justice. In doing so, know that, while you certainly will not solve the crises of the world, you will be of help; and that's a good thing.

Appendix:
Summary of Elemental Practice

Embedded in the chapters on the Five Elements are suggestions for elemental contemplative practice. Here is a summary of these practical suggestions. Each element will be accompanied by activities to develop your relationship to that element as well as some reflection questions to assist you in noticing both the neurotic and the wisdom manifestations of the element.

PREPARING FOR ELEMENTAL PRACTICE

It is helpful to begin elemental practice time with a period of silent prayer. This prayer helps to develop our awareness and attention. There are a number of silent prayer/contemplation techniques, including Centering Prayer, Breathing Prayer, and the Body Scan. Here is a brief description of the Centering Prayer technique.

As with all contemplative practices, it's essential to understand that there is no incorrect form. You cannot pray in the wrong way! Many people cease practicing contemplative prayer because they believe there is something wrong with their technique. This isn't true. The purpose of any prayer practice isn't to "be spiritual" or to "quiet your mind" but rather to pay attention and, when your mind wanders and becomes distracted, return to your practice. That is all. You will have numerous thoughts, feelings, and distractions, all of which are perfectly normal. Recognizing that you cannot practice incorrectly is part of developing the compassion and loving kindness that are the heart of your elemental practice.

In Centering Prayer, you choose a word that is used to help you return to the present moment whenever your mind wanders off. Although some people call this a "sacred word," it doesn't matter which word you choose, so don't worry or spend much time in picking one. Think of the word as a ship's anchor. The anchor allows the ship to float and move in a small area, but keeps it from drifting off to sea.

In silent prayer, it is helpful to decide how long you will pray and set a timer. Fifteen or twenty minutes is a good starting point, but if you have only five or ten minutes, that's fine too. First, note your intention to focus and surrender yourself to God. Sit upright in a comfortable position with hands on your lap and feet on the floor. Your eyes can be open or closed. If open, it is helpful to have your gaze downward, hitting the floor a few feet in front of you, and be mindful of your experience, your thoughts, feelings, and bodily sensations. When you notice that your attention drifts, say your word silently and refocus. That's it!

These few minutes of silent prayer can then be followed by a period of elemental reflection. If you don't have the time or inclination to pray silently before your elemental practice, simply approach your elemental reflection time as openly as possible. During your practice, bring your awareness to your thoughts, your feelings, and your bodily sensations. What do you notice?

- What is the content of your thoughts? Are there particular things you think about when relating to each element?

- How do your thoughts "feel"? Are they sharp and precise or dull and vague? Get to know the experience of your mind in relation to each element.

- You can ask the same set of questions regarding your feelings. What feelings arise in relation to each element? What is their content and focus? What is their energetic quality?

- Finally, notice how each elemental energy is experienced in your body. Are you hungry when doing earth practice? Does your vision sharpen when you engage the water element?

Elemental practice is enhanced by creative expression. At the end of your elemental practice, take time to journal, draw, or engage in some other form of creativity that highlights your observations of the elemental energy.

Being aware of our experience helps us to develop a better picture of how we respond to the qualities of each element, both the wisdom *and* the neurotic qualities. This awareness allows us to move toward the wisdom aspect of that elemental energy in daily life.

The Space Element

- If you have access to a place where there is a lot of open space, spend time wandering there. If not, use pictures on your computer, from a nature book, or, finally, if you have been to a wide open space, spend time recalling and visualizing that experience.

- As you spend time contemplating the element of space, allow your mind and body to expand. Notice what spaciousness feels like and your reaction to this element. Practice breathing.

- Is your mind dull or open? Do you withdraw from space or embrace it? Do you instinctively want to fill the space or can you relax in the openness?

- Throughout your day, become aware of how you relate to open space. What thoughts and feelings emerge when you have free time, free space? Are they pleasant or stressful?

- Notice your relationship to social space. Are you comfortable "taking up space," or do you prefer to disappear in space? Practice relaxing into your own spaciousness. Practice compassionately taking up space.

- Practice listening and "holding space" in group situations. How do you react? Do you tend to jump in and respond quickly, or can you sit and be open to others interacting in the space? What is it like for you to practicing equanimity: simply being and not doing?

- Spend time with the color white: a white room, a blank sheet of white paper, a white wall. What are your reactions?

- Notice when you ignore thoughts, feelings, people, and situations. Is there anything or anyone in the space you are trying to avoid? How might you encourage yourself to attend to these things?

- Practice creative expression in response to your reflections.

The Water Element

- Spend time relating directly to water, either in person or through a picture or video. This practice could be outdoors or inside with a water feature, fountain, while bathing, or even just a pretty bowl full of water. Focus on your thoughts, feelings, and bodily sensations.

- Spend time with the color blue. Notice your reactions.

- What is your relationship with clarity? When do you appreciate clarity, and when do you avoid it?

- Spend time with music or art that is precise, crisp, and clear. What do you notice?

- What is your emotional state when things in your life are unclear, chaotic, or confused? How do you react?

- Notice your relationship with anger. Do you avoid the clarity of anger, or do you use anger to get your way and force others to agree with you?

- What is your relationship with clarity in social spaces? Do you help bring clarity to situations at work or other social spaces? How do you feel when others bring clarity? Is it soothing or irritating?

- What is your relationship to rules? Do you find them helpful or confining? Are you rigid about rules, or do you use them as useful guides?

- As you go through your day and reflect on the landscape of your life, ask yourself: What parts of myself and my life need watering?

- Practice creative expression in response to your reflections.

THE AIR ELEMENT

- Spend time becoming aware of the air you breathe. This can be inside or outside. You might also look at pictures of landscapes where you imagine the air is fresh and clean.

- Watch a stop-action video of flowers blooming or new growth sprouting.

- Spend time with the color green.

- Observe your reactions to wind. Stand out in variable wind conditions. When do you enjoy a nice breeze, and when would you rather be indoors?

- Notice your relationship to action. Are you very busy? Do you like the pace of your life, or would you prefer to slow down? What are your feelings regarding action? Are you irritable? Are you often forcing others to move at your pace? What is it like for you to do nothing?

- Practice discernment. Reflecting on your day or week, ask yourself: What are life-giving actions? What actions are death dealing? Can you answer these questions with increasing indifference so that you discern your answers more clearly? What do the answers tell you about where the Spirit is blowing in your life?

- In social spaces, observe your relationship to action. Do you want to act quickly, without much reflection time? Can you slow down and listen more deeply for an action that might be more fruitful? Do you ever feel that you are "running around like a chicken without its head"? What would help you to slow down?

- What is your level of comfort with movement? Does activity make you nervous, comfortable, happy, or distressed?

- Practice creative expression in response to your reflections. For this element, you could try a movement activity or do a dance in your living room.

The Earth Element

- Spend time in direct relationship to the earth. Take a walk and focus on your feet on the ground. Lie on the earth. Lean against rocks or large trees. Feel the solidity of your body. Be aware of gravity.

- Spend time with the color yellow and with pictures or videos of the earth. Watch the television series *Planet Earth*.

- Notice your relationship with food. Eat slowly and be conscious of the nourishment you are receiving. What is your relationship to cooking? Practice cooking a meal for yourself, your family, and your friends. What is this experience like?

- Do you feel a sense of abundance or poverty in your life? Do you feel that you have enough, or are you always grasping for more? What would be enough?

- Spend time in environments that are well appointed or full of color and texture. If you don't have access to any such environments in private settings seek them out in museums. What is this experience like for you?

- Identify your sense of taste and style? Do you enjoy nice things, or do you have little care for material possessions?

- In social situations, what is your relationship to care and nurture? Are you drawn toward providing for others? Do you care about the earth and environmental issues? Are you a "helper" and "nurturer"?

- What is your reaction when others help you? Can you receive help, or do you reject it? What happens when someone compliments you? Do you accept or reject this attention?

- Practice creative expression in response to your reflections.

The Fire Element

- Spend time relating directly to the element of fire. This could be a campfire, a fire in your fireplace, a candle, or a picture or video of fire. As with the other elements, you could also spend time remembering a positive experience of fire, visualizing and reliving the experience.

- Spend time with the color red.

- Notice the state of relationships in your life. Where is there openness, love, or vulnerability? Which relationships are cold or superficial? How do you feel about these observations?

- What is your relationship to feelings in general? Are you aware of your feelings? Do you avoid feelings? Are you afraid of them, or do you embrace them? Are they important to you?

- How do you relate to yourself? Do you love and appreciate who you are, or do you spend time "beating yourself up" and directing negativity toward yourself?

- In social spaces, notice how you relate to others, especially those who are different from you. Can you extend love toward those you do not understand? Do you see the "other" as human or as something less than human? How do you react to injustice in the world?

- Focus on your heart. Are you aware of your heart space? How does that feel? Can you notice its warmth, or does it feel closed and cold? What is this awareness like for you?

- Practice the loving-kindness meditation.
- Practice creative expression in response to your reflections.

While elemental practice can be done individually, it is valuable to do these practices in a group setting, sharing your reflections with the group. Perhaps you could start an elemental practice group at your church!

Always remember: practice with loving kindness and compassion for yourself and for the world.

KEY SCRIPTURE REFERENCES

Space: Genesis 1:2; Proverbs 9:1–6; Revelation 1:8; 2 Samuel 7:12–17

Water: John 4:13–14; Proverbs 29:18 (KJV); Genesis 1:20–22; Proverbs 1:2–6

Air: John 3:8; Genesis 1:2; Psalm 127:1

Earth: Genesis 2:7; Matthew 14:14–21; Exodus 16:15; Acts 2:44–46

Fire: Matthew 3:11; 1 John 4:8; Malachi 3:1–3; John 13:34–35; Matthew 5:43–48

Chart: Summary of the Five Wisdom System

The following chart provides a summary of the Five Elements, their wisdom and neurotic aspects, as well as their associated color, season, ego-style, and realm.

Element	Wisdom Aspect	Neurotic Aspect	Color	Season	Ego-Style Realm
Space	Equanimity Radical acceptance Spacious hospitality	Ignoring Dullness of mind Disconnect from reality	White	All seasons	Ignorance God and animal realm
Water	Clarity Mirror-like wisdom Vision	Judgment Arrogance Arguing over ideas	Blue	Winter	Aggression Jealous gods
Air	Compassionate and wise action Action and stillness are valued	Action for its own sake Anxiety War	Green	Spring	Aggression Hell realm
Earth	Abundance Generosity There is always enough	Sense of poverty Never enough Grasping	Yellow	Fall	Passion Hungry ghosts
Fire	Love Wise relationships Warmth	Deep insecurity Relationship dysfunction Loneliness	Red	Summer	Passion Human realm